I0605122
TO:
FROM:
DATE:

Visit Christian Art Gifts, Inc., at www.christianartgifts.com.

Praying the Promises of God: A 52-Week Guided Prayer Journal

Published by Christian Art Gifts, Inc., Bloomingdale, IL, USA.

Published in association with Mary DeMuth Literary, mary@marydemuthliterary.com.

First edition 2025.

Designed by Christian Art Gifts, Inc.

Cover and interior images used under license from Shutterstock.com.

Most Christian Art titles may be purchased at bulk discounts by churches, nonprofits, and corporations. For more information, please email SpecialMarkets@cagifts.com.

ISBN: 978-1-63952-905-6

Printed in Vietnam.

30 29 28 27 26 25
11 10 9 8 7 6 5 4 3 2

Praying THE PROMISES OF GOD

52-WEEK GUIDED PRAYER JOURNAL

RACHEL WOJO

A NOTE FROM THE AUTHOR

Dear Friend,

Life can be harsh. The situations and circumstances we experience often force us to reach for something larger than ourselves. Life's challenges drive us to seek comfort in God's promises. Thankfully, we can cling to them.

God's Word is full of His promises to us. According to BibleInfo.com, it has been estimated that there are 3,573 promises in the Bible, and other sources have cited as many as 7,000! What incredible assurance from our heavenly Father.

From our first acceptance of salvation to our last breath on earth, knowing what God says to be true provides confidence in our Creator.

Restating promises to God in prayer strengthens our belief. God will do what He says He will do. Holding fast to His declarations promotes joy in our hearts.

Praying God's promises is a beautiful expression of prayer. When we carefully focus our attention on the promises of God's Word, we find the cares and worries of our hearts melting into His confidence and peace. Your God has never broken a promise. Rest in that.

When God makes a promise, He never changes His mind. When we pray, we can remind Him of His promises and express our gratitude when they are fulfilled. Praying God's promises is a beautiful way to communicate with Him and give Him glory. By reminding God of His promises, we remind ourselves of His faithfulness.

God's promises are unchanging and always true. That's why I created the *Praying the Promises of God* which identifies fifty-two promises of God that we can pray confidently.

Are you ready to join me on this journey of knowing and praying God's promises? I hope you are!

By His grace,

Rachel

GUIDE TO USING THIS JOURNAL

Your *Praying the Promises of God* includes six different weekly sections:

Read

Meditate on the key Bible verse and read an additional passage for context. The longer passage is included at the end of the weekly sections so that you can easily return to it throughout the week.

Remember

Think about God's promise from the key Bible verse and what it means.

Reflect

Enjoy this space as a place to record your response to the devotion. Record your thoughts or the main idea. Or you could write or rewrite the key verse.

Journal

Write the date so you can track how God moves throughout the year. Include thoughts about how you've seen God at work and how He has answered prayers. This is *your* journal, so use this space as you'd like.

Pray

Pray God's promise in a personal way. Write a prayer for yourself or for others that is based on the weekly promise. Or simply use this space to keep a record of the things you are lifting up in prayer.

Praise

Praise God for His promise and for keeping all His promises. You can also use this space to record the ways in which God has answered your prayers.

Week One

"Never will I leave you; never will I forsake you."

HEBREWS 13:5

Read

Hebrews 13:5–8

Remember

God promises He will never leave me.

Reflect

Aren't you thankful for the promise that God will never abandon you? Do you feel afraid and perhaps like God is nowhere to be found? Sometimes fear can irrationally grip our hearts. However, God has promised never to leave us alone. Since He is our helper, there is no need for us to be afraid. He promises to remain by our side always, while our responsibility is to have no fear and to trust in Him. We sometimes fail to pray God's promises because we struggle to trust them. Make today's promise the confidence you need to trust Him completely.

Father, help me to know that You are always near.

Journal

How does fear prevent me from fully believing God's promises?

Pray

Praise

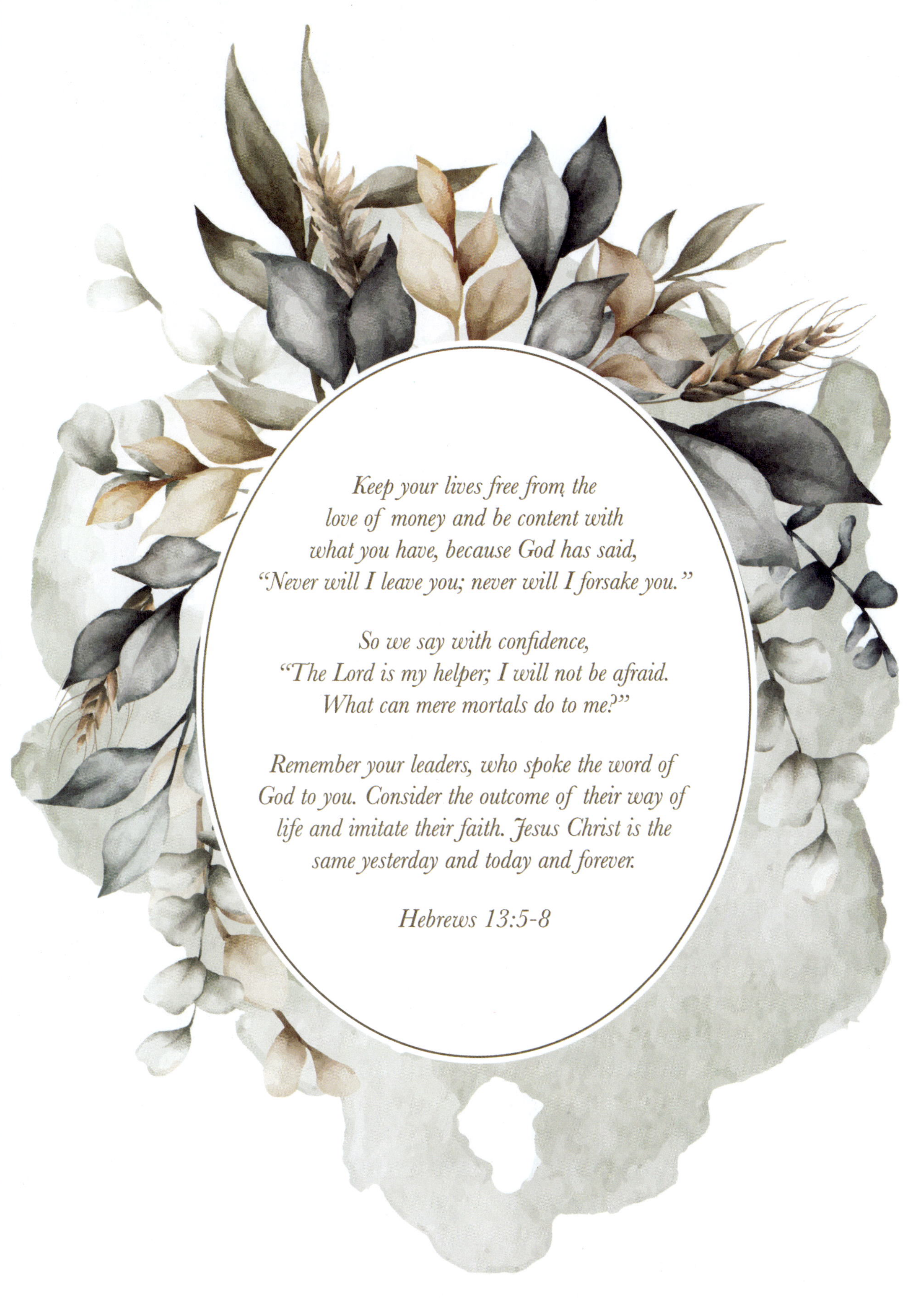

Keep your lives free from the
love of money and be content with
what you have, because God has said,
"Never will I leave you; never will I forsake you."

So we say with confidence,
"The Lord is my helper; I will not be afraid.
What can mere mortals do to me?"

Remember your leaders, who spoke the word of
God to you. Consider the outcome of their way of
life and imitate their faith. Jesus Christ is the
same yesterday and today and forever.

Hebrews 13:5-8

Week Two
Who shall
separate us from
the Love
of Christ?
ROMANS 8:35 ESV

Read

Romans 8:35–39

Remember

God promises that nothing will separate me from His love.

Reflect

Life is full of challenges, from distress and persecution to disease and death. However, this comforting verse promises us that nothing can separate us from God's love. His love transcends any problem and, because of His love that conquered the grave, we can overcome even the toughest obstacles. Romans 8:35 ensures our survival and transforms us into conquerors, giving us the resilience and courage to face life's complexities head-on. By viewing every trial through God's unfailing love, we can recognize that His love is both a shield and a conquering force. He is enabling you to navigate life's adversities with confidence and strength.

Father, help me to remember that You have given me the power to conquer all things because Your love is greater than all.

Journal

What problem am I struggling with that God's immense love has overcome?

Pray

Praise

Who shall separate us from the love of Christ?
Shall tribulation, or distress, or persecution, or famine,
or nakedness, or danger, or sword? As it is written,

"For your sake we are being killed all the day long;
we are regarded as sheep to be slaughtered."

No, in all these things we are more than conquerors through him who loved us. For I am sure that neither death nor life, nor angels nor rulers, nor things present nor things to come, nor powers, nor height nor depth, nor anything else in all creation, will be able to separate us from the love of God in Christ Jesus our Lord.

Romans 8:35-39 ESV

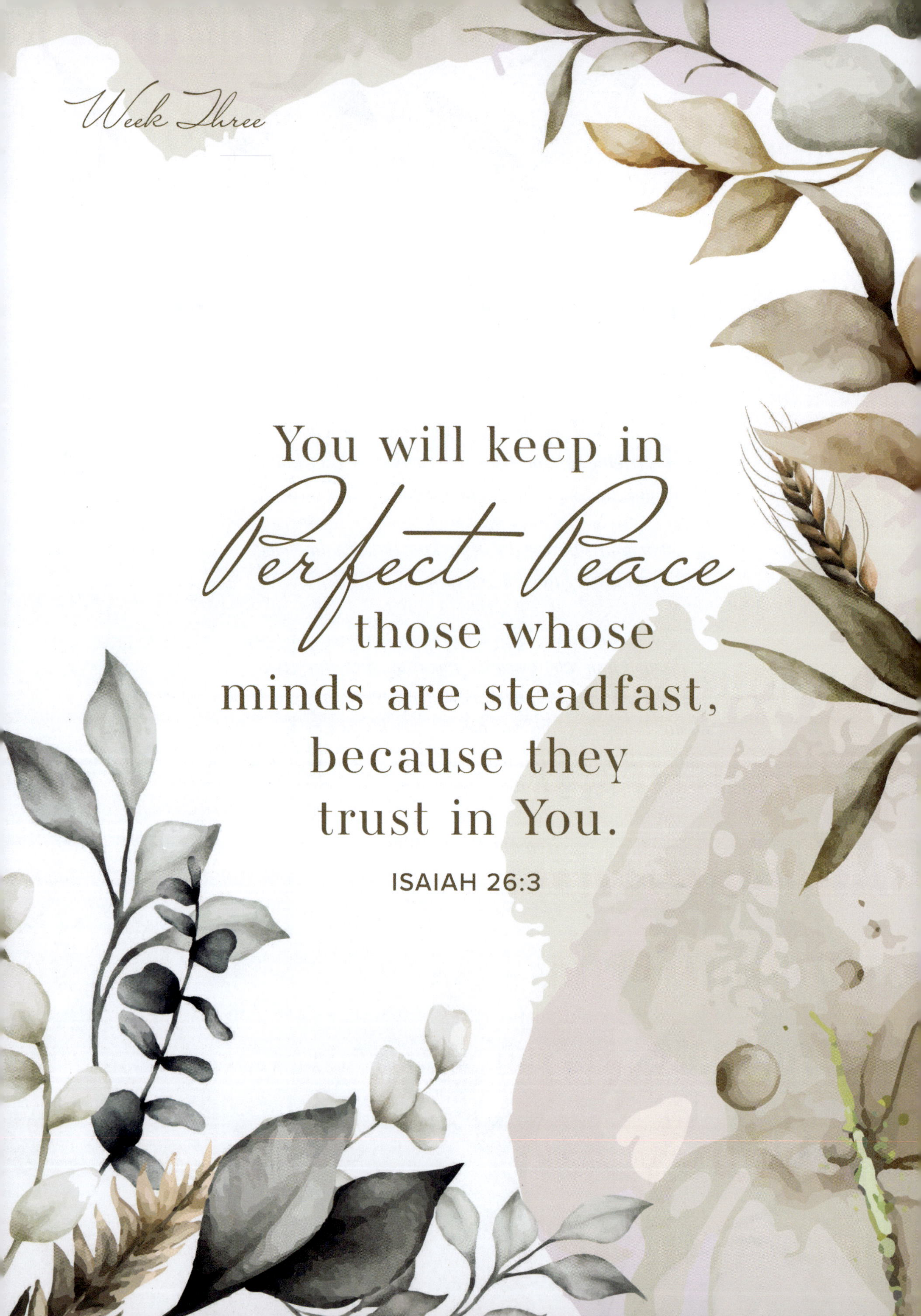

Week Three

You will keep in
Perfect Peace
those whose
minds are steadfast,
because they
trust in You.

ISAIAH 26:3

Read

Isaiah 26:1–10

Remember

God promises to keep my mind in perfect peace when I trust Him.

Reflect

When life's walls start to crumble, our thoughts often crumble too. The adversary aims to shatter our peace, yet believing God gives roots to our tranquility and grants us a resilient mindset. Entrusting ourselves to the promise that peace is under God's control, we can confidently embrace a steadfast state of mind. Sheila Walsh beautifully articulates, "Peace isn't the absence of trouble but the presence of Christ." Welcoming this truth allows us to trust that peace is His gift, freely offered to us amid life's challenges. His peace is available to you at this moment if you choose to release your life to Him.

Father, I trust You and long for Your peace to blanket my heart.

Journal

How can you practice trusting in God's promise of peace during moments or seasons of adversity?

Pray

Praise

We have a strong city;
God makes salvation its walls and ramparts.
Open the gates that the righteous nation may enter,
the nation that keeps faith.
You will keep in perfect peace those whose minds are steadfast,
because they trust in you.
Trust in the LORD forever,
for the LORD, the LORD himself, is the Rock eternal.
He humbles those who dwell on high, he lays the lofty city low;
he levels it to the ground and casts it down to the dust.
Feet trample it down—
the feet of the oppressed,
the footsteps of the poor.

The path of the righteous is level;
you, the Upright One, make the way of the righteous smooth.
Yes, LORD, walking in the way of your laws, we wait for you;
your name and renown are the desire of our hearts.
My soul yearns for you in the night;
in the morning my spirit longs for you.
When your judgments come upon the earth,
the people of the world learn righteousness.
But when grace is shown to the wicked,
they do not learn righteousness;
even in a land of uprightness they go on doing evil
and do not regard the majesty of the LORD.

Isaiah 26:1-10

Week Four
Be strong and Courageous
Do not be afraid;
do not be discouraged,
for the LORD your God
will be with you
wherever you go.
JOSHUA 1:9

Read

Joshua 1:1–9

Remember

God promises to be with me wherever I go.

Reflect

God promises to be with you always, never abandoning you. It is incredible to know that God accompanies us on every step of our journey, offering unwavering support. He never abandons us to navigate life on our own. However, we often forget our role in this divine partnership. God instructs us to banish fear and discouragement. We can't allow fear or discouragement to be closer to our hearts than this promise. Clinging to the blessed assurance of His constant, comforting presence allows us to face challenges without fear and find courage in His company. Let's seek His strength to truly embrace this promise.

Father, give me renewed strength and courage to remember Your presence.

Journal

How many times does "be strong and courageous" appear in Joshua 1:1–9, and what does this mean to me?

Pray

Praise

After the death of Moses the servant of the LORD, the LORD said to Joshua son of Nun, Moses' aide: "Moses my servant is dead. Now then, you and all these people, get ready to cross the Jordan River into the land I am about to give to them—to the Israelites. I will give you every place where you set your foot, as I promised Moses. Your territory will extend from the desert to Lebanon, and from the great river, the Euphrates—all the Hittite country—to the Mediterranean Sea in the west. No one will be able to stand against you all the days of your life. As I was with Moses, so I will be with you; I will never leave you nor forsake you. Be strong and courageous, because you will lead these people to inherit the land I swore to their ancestors to give them.

"Be strong and very courageous. Be careful to obey all the law my servant Moses gave you; do not turn from it to the right or to the left, that you may be successful wherever you go. Keep this Book of the Law always on your lips; meditate on it day and night, so that you may be careful to do everything written in it. Then you will be prosperous and successful. Have I not commanded you? Be strong and courageous. Do not be afraid; do not be discouraged, for the LORD your God will be with you wherever you go."

Joshua 1:1-9

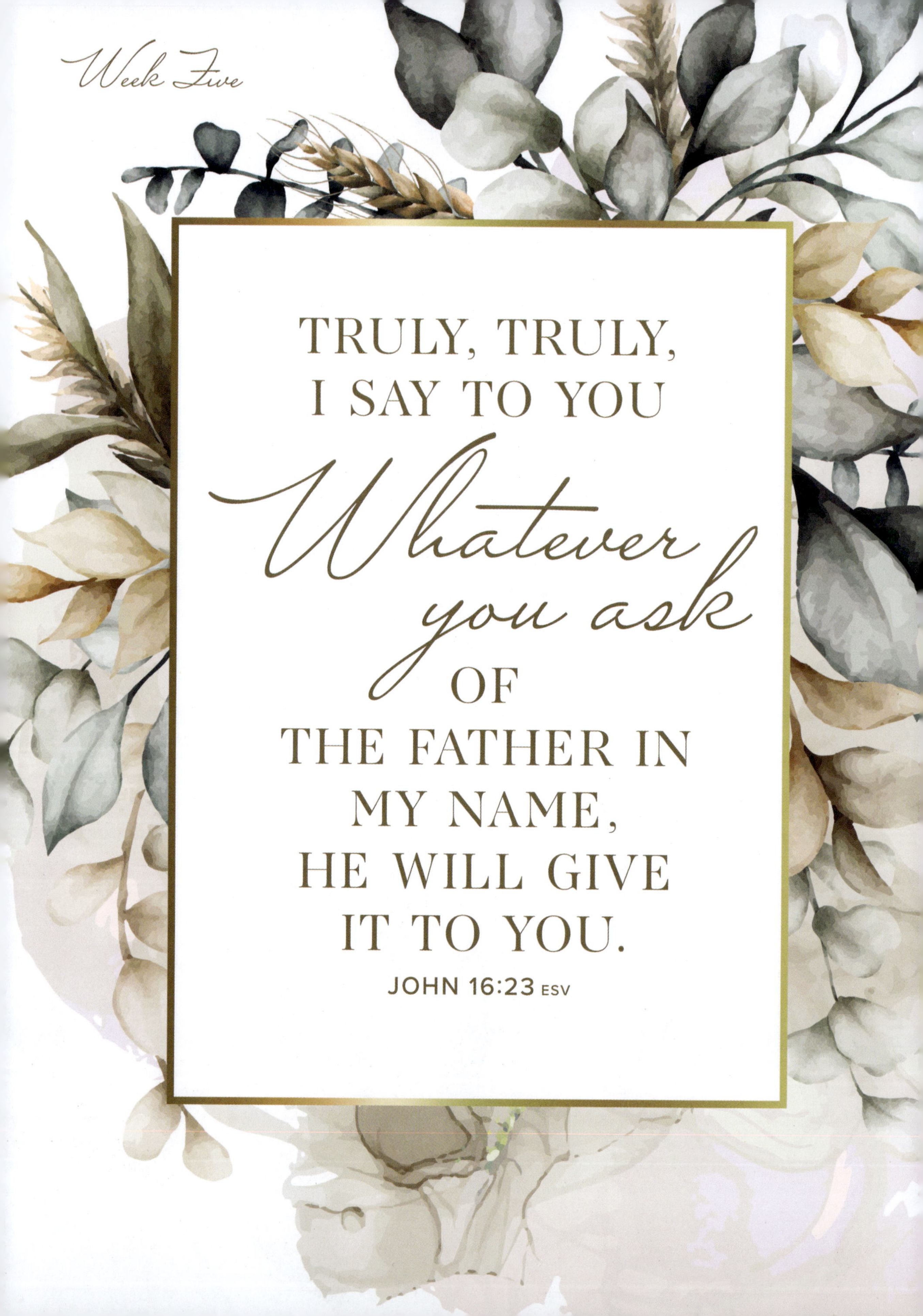

Week Five
TRULY, TRULY,
I SAY TO YOU
Whatever
you ask
OF
THE FATHER IN
MY NAME,
HE WILL GIVE
IT TO YOU.
JOHN 16:23 ESV

Read

John 16:23–33

Remember

God promises that if I ask, He will provide.

Reflect

It is incredible to imagine that one day in the future, we won't have any need for food, clothing, or shelter. Instead, heaven will be all we need! However, until that day, Jesus instructed His disciples to ask their Father for anything. He also promised that whatever we ask for in Jesus' name, the Father will give us. This invitation to seek provision directly from our Heavenly Father addresses our immediate struggles and fosters a deep and trusting connection with Him. It highlights our intimate relationship with Him, where our requests are met with loving care. We can find comfort in knowing that no matter how small or large, we can find help through our connection with the ever-loving Father.

Father, I ask, in Jesus' name, that You would provide.

Journal

What is the most pressing need I long for God to fill?

Pray

Praise

"In that day you will ask nothing of me. Truly, truly, I say to you, whatever you ask of the Father in my name, he will give it to you. Until now you have asked nothing in my name. Ask, and you will receive, that your joy may be full.

"I have said these things to you in figures of speech. The hour is coming when I will no longer speak to you in figures of speech but will tell you plainly about the Father. In that day you will ask in my name, and I do not say to you that I will ask the Father on your behalf; for the Father himself loves you, because you have loved me and have believed that I came from God. I came from the Father and have come into the world, and now I am leaving the world and going to the Father."

His disciples said, "Ah, now you are speaking plainly and not using figurative speech! Now we know that you know all things and do not need anyone to question you; this is why we believe that you came from God." Jesus answered them, "Do you now believe? Behold, the hour is coming, indeed it has come, when you will be scattered, each to his own home, and will leave me alone. Yet I am not alone, for the Father is with me. I have said these things to you, that in me you may have peace. In the world you will have tribulation. But take heart; I have overcome the world."

John 16:23-33 ESV

Week Six

YOU ARE
MY
hiding place
YOU WILL PROTECT ME
FROM TROUBLE
AND SURROUND ME
WITH SONGS OF
DELIVERANCE.

PSALM 32:7

Read

Psalm 32:6–11

Remember

God promises His loving devotion will surround me when I trust Him.

Reflect

Living with uncertainty can be a challenging experience. Illnesses and accidents can occur to anyone, at any time, without warning. Such unpredictable circumstances make us unsure about ourselves and our future. Sometimes we may even question God's plan for us. However, Psalm 32 offers a ray of hope by explaining that God promises to guide us and show us the way forward. His love enfolds us, providing us with peace and protection, no matter what challenges we may face.

Father, thank You for surrounding me. Expand my trust in Your love.

Journal

How can I embrace my Father as He surrounds my present circumstances?

Pray

Praise

Therefore let all the faithful pray
to you while you may be found;
surely the rising of the mighty
waters will not reach them.
You are my hiding place;
you will protect me from trouble
and surround me with songs of deliverance.

I will instruct you and teach you in the way you should go;
I will counsel you with my loving eye on you.
Do not be like the horse or the mule,
which have no understanding
but must be controlled by bit and bridle
or they will not come to you.
Many are the woes of the wicked,
but the Lord*'s unfailing love*
surrounds the one who trusts in him.

Rejoice in the Lord *and be glad, you righteous;*
sing, all you who are upright in heart!

Psalm 32:6-11

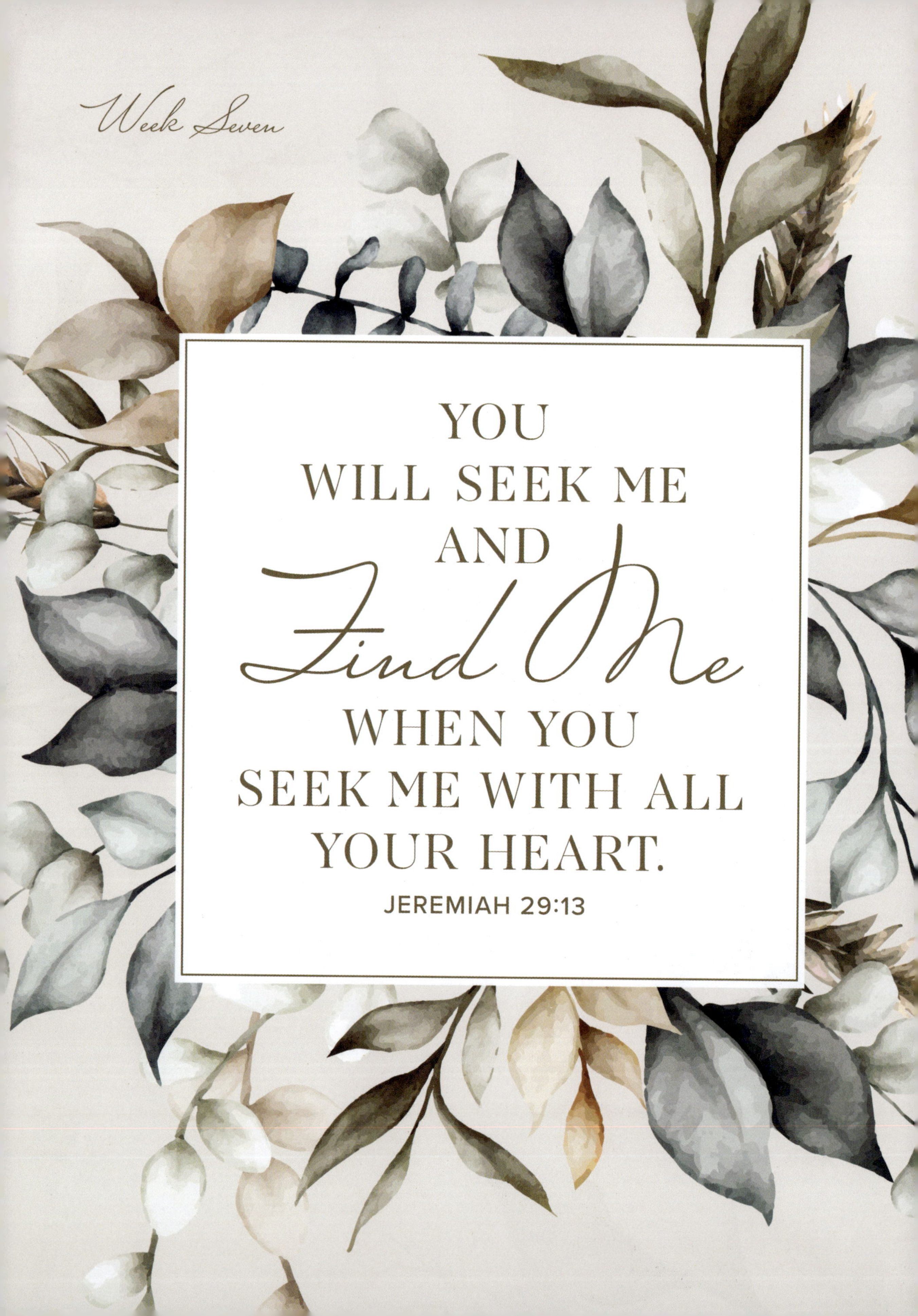
Week Seven
YOU
WILL SEEK ME
AND
Find Me
WHEN YOU
SEEK ME WITH ALL
YOUR HEART.
JEREMIAH 29:13

Read

Jeremiah 29:10–14

Remember

God promises I will find Him when I seek Him.

Reflect

In today's passage, Jeremiah shares the Word of the Lord with the exiles living in Babylon. He assures them that God will deliver them when the time is right, but until then, they should live their lives to the fullest. God promises to give them a future and hope. He pledges to answer them when they call on Him and be there for them when they seek Him. This promise is not limited to the exiles but extends to us today. God's willingness to be found is a timeless assurance that transcends historical contexts. No matter our circumstances, we can find God and follow Him into the hopeful future He promises.

Father, I am searching for You. Reveal Yourself to me.

Journal

How can I trust God's promise of a hopeful future? How can I seek Him in my current circumstances?

Pray

Praise

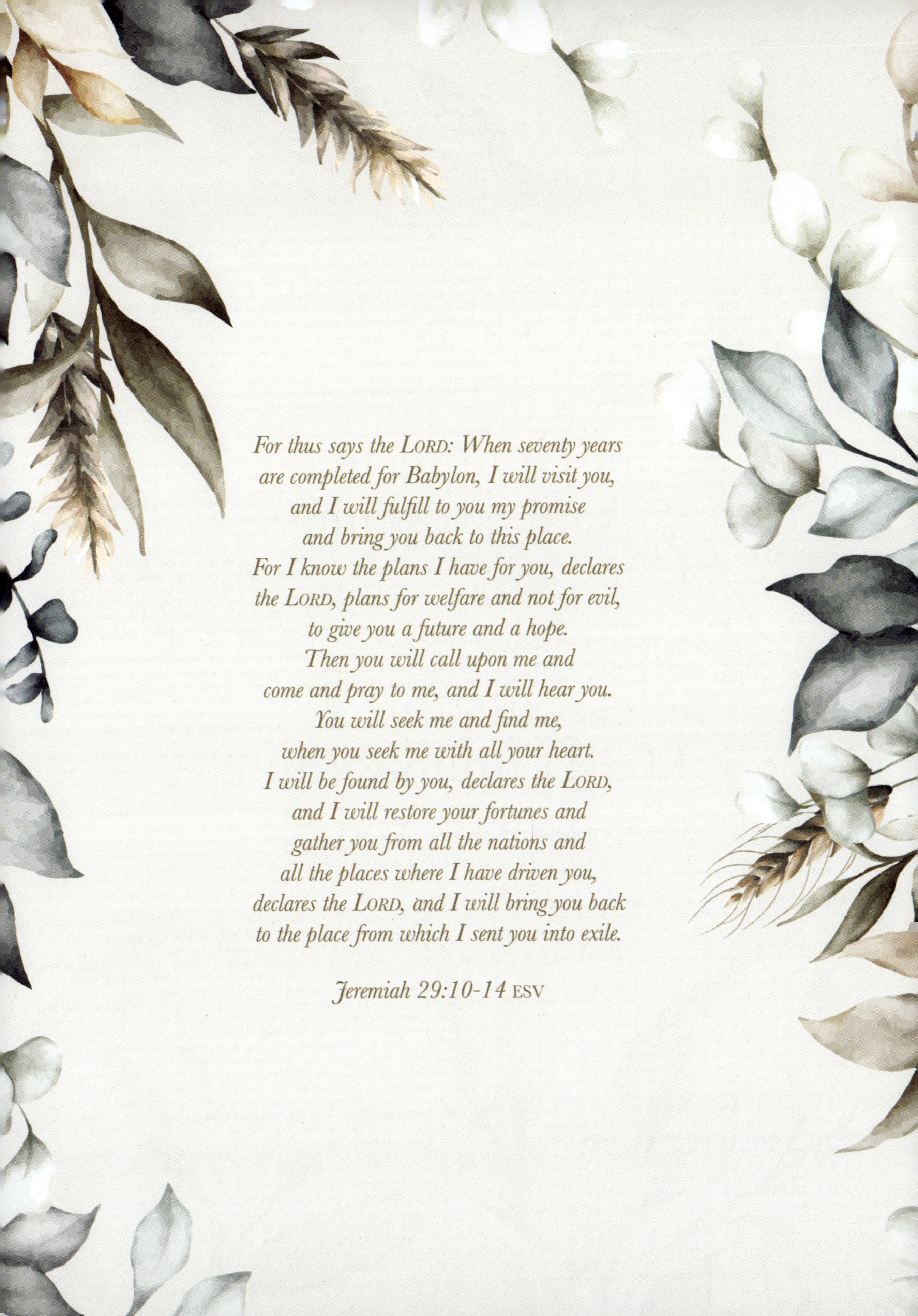

For thus says the Lord*: When seventy years*
are completed for Babylon, I will visit you,
and I will fulfill to you my promise
and bring you back to this place.
For I know the plans I have for you, declares
the Lord*, plans for welfare and not for evil,*
to give you a future and a hope.
Then you will call upon me and
come and pray to me, and I will hear you.
You will seek me and find me,
when you seek me with all your heart.
I will be found by you, declares the Lord*,*
and I will restore your fortunes and
gather you from all the nations and
all the places where I have driven you,
declares the Lord*, and I will bring you back*
to the place from which I sent you into exile.

Jeremiah 29:10-14 ESV

Week Eight
Though he
may stumble,
He will not fall
for the
LORD upholds him
with His hand.
PSALM 37:24

Read

Psalm 37:23–24

Remember

God promises that He holds my hand when I'm overwhelmed.

Reflect

Even in our weakest moments, we can find comfort in the fact that God's unwavering presence sustains us. When the tumbles of life threaten to overtake us, His hand remains a steady anchor, ensuring we never face our problems alone. Embrace the promise that, in our vulnerability, God is our refuge, holding us securely. Remember that your Creator is intimately involved in every step of your journey, promising to not only hold you above the waves, but also to cradle you in His safe arms.

Father, let me feel the strength of Your hand holding mine.

Journal

What details in my current environment challenge me to remember that God is both cradling me and holding me up?

Pray

Praise

The Lord directs the steps of the godly.
He delights in every detail of their lives.
Though they stumble, they will never fall,
for the Lord holds them by the hand.

Psalm 37:23-24 NLT

Week Nine

Do not be anxious
about anything,
but in every situation,
by
Prayer & Petition
— with —
thanksgiving,
present your
requests to God.

PHILIPPIANS 4:6

Read

Philippians 4:6–10

Remember

God promises incomprehensible peace when I pray.

Reflect

"Do not be anxious about anything." One might think avoiding anxiety is easier said than done, but Paul guides us on how to do it. He advises us to present our requests to God instead of giving in to anxiety. What happens when we pray? God's peace, beyond our understanding, will guard our hearts. Praying for God's promises to be fulfilled will bring peace to our lives. Moreover, presenting our concerns to God is not just a transaction but an invitation to cultivate a profound relationship with the Almighty. It's a practice that allows us to exchange anxiety for a peace that goes beyond our understanding. By taking our concerns to God, we create a peaceful sanctuary within our hearts that is shielded by His reassuring presence.

Father, calm my anxious heart.

Journal

Where do I need to allow God's peace to sink deeper into my soul?

Pray

Praise

*Do not be anxious about anything,
but in everything by prayer and supplication
with thanksgiving let your requests be made
known to God. And the peace of God,
which surpasses all understanding,
will guard your hearts and
your minds in Christ Jesus.*

*Finally, brothers, whatever is true,
whatever is honorable, whatever is just,
whatever is pure, whatever is lovely,
whatever is commendable,
if there is any excellence,
if there is anything worthy of praise,
think about these things.
What you have learned and received
and heard and seen in me—practice
these things, and the God of
peace will be with you.*

*I rejoiced in the Lord greatly that now at
length you have revived your concern for me.
You were indeed concerned for me,
but you had no opportunity.*

Philippians 4:6-10 ESV

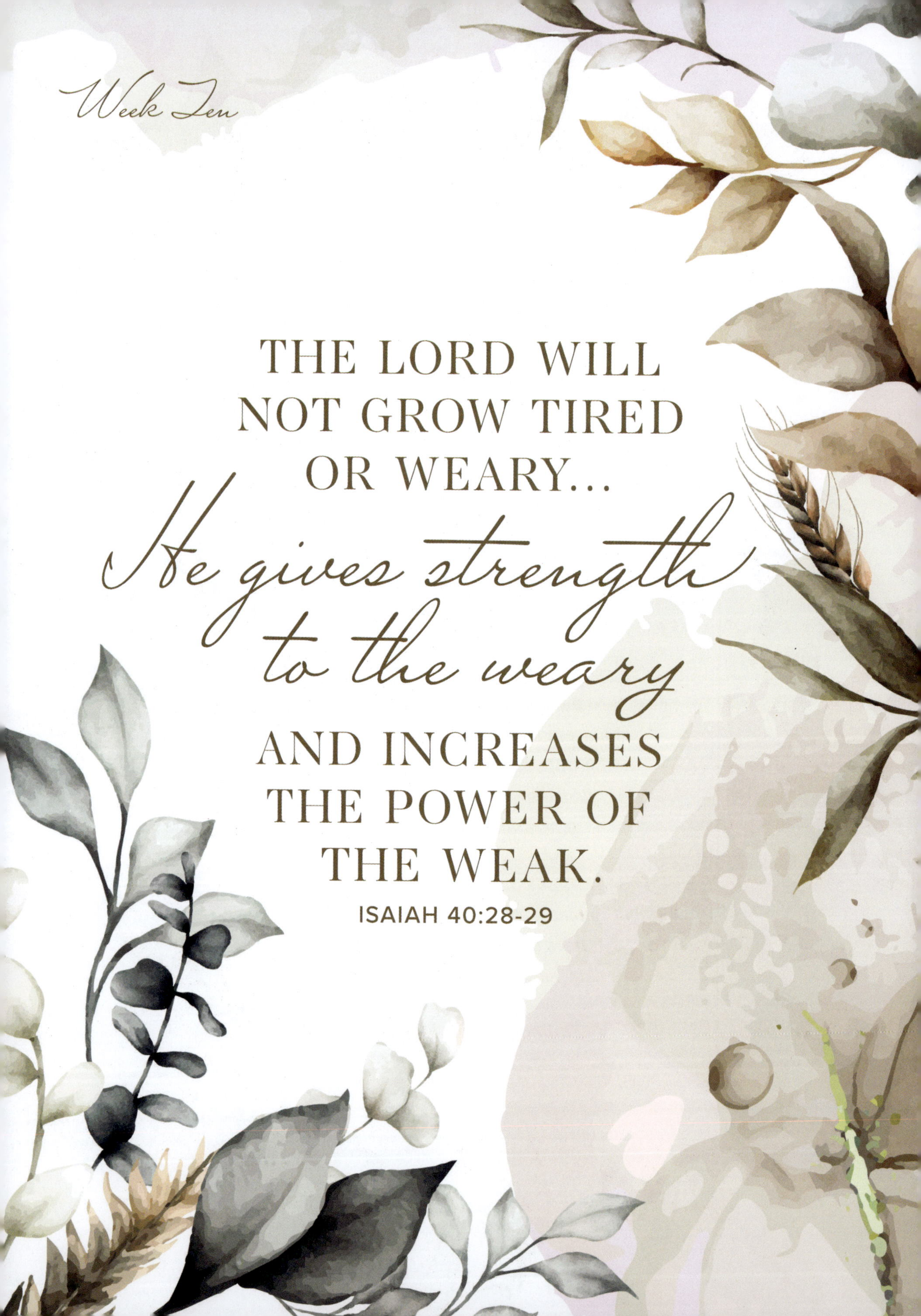

Week Ten

THE LORD WILL
NOT GROW TIRED
OR WEARY...
He gives strength
to the weary
AND INCREASES
THE POWER OF
THE WEAK.

ISAIAH 40:28-29

Read

Isaiah 40:28–31

Remember

God promises to give me the strength I need for today.

Reflect

Whenever we see a portion of Scripture that says, "God will," we can look for the promises of what He declares He will do. In today's key verse, God promises never to grow tired or weary (which is hard for me to imagine!) and to give power and increase strength. What happens when we allow God to do His part? We are renewed, refreshed, restored, and ready to do His will. This promise is a divine exchange that replaces our weariness with His unwavering strength. Embracing this promise isn't just about receiving a boost, it's about experiencing a profound transformation. As we allow God to infuse us with His power, we find ourselves restored and revitalized, ready to embark on His purpose with newfound vigor and resilience.

Father, infuse me with the strength only You can give.

Journal

Where do I need strength for life that only God can give?

Pray

Praise

Do you not know?
Have you not heard?
The LORD is the everlasting God,
the Creator of the ends of the earth.
He will not grow tired or weary,
and his understanding no one can fathom.
He gives strength to the weary
and increases the power of the weak.
Even youths grow tired and weary,
and young men stumble and fall;
but those who hope in the LORD
will renew their strength.
They will soar on wings like eagles;
they will run and not grow weary,
they will walk and not be faint.
Isaiah 40:28-31

Week Eleven

WHEN YOU
PASS THROUGH
THE WATERS,

I will be with you

AND WHEN
YOU PASS THROUGH
THE RIVERS,
THEY WILL NOT
SWEEP OVER YOU.

ISAIAH 43:2

Read

Isaiah 43:1–12

Remember

God promises when I pass through the waters, He will be with me.

Reflect

Isaiah 43:1–12 describes God's promises to Jacob and the children of Israel, which are still relevant today. We can appreciate that God doesn't say "if," but "when" we pass through troubled waters. However, we don't have to be overwhelmed by our challenges because God is always with us, offering support and guidance. The promise extends beyond just surviving challenges. God assures us that His presence will help us navigate through the difficulties of life and transform them into opportunities for growth and resilience. You can find comfort in His presence and peace in this promise today.

Father, help me to trust that there is purpose in these troubled waters.

Journal

How does God's presence lift you from the choppiness of the waters you're walking this week?

Pray

Praise

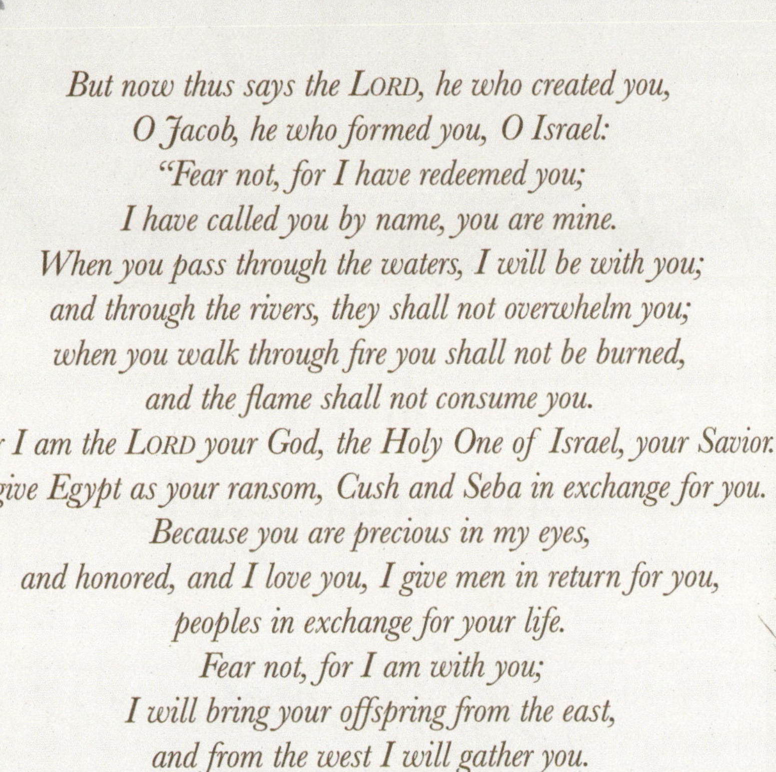

But now thus says the Lord, he who created you,
O Jacob, he who formed you, O Israel:
"Fear not, for I have redeemed you;
I have called you by name, you are mine.
When you pass through the waters, I will be with you;
and through the rivers, they shall not overwhelm you;
when you walk through fire you shall not be burned,
and the flame shall not consume you.
For I am the Lord your God, the Holy One of Israel, your Savior.
I give Egypt as your ransom, Cush and Seba in exchange for you.
Because you are precious in my eyes,
and honored, and I love you, I give men in return for you,
peoples in exchange for your life.
Fear not, for I am with you;
I will bring your offspring from the east,
and from the west I will gather you.
I will say to the north, Give up,
and to the south, Do not withhold; bring my sons
from afar and my daughters from the end of the earth,
everyone who is called by my name,
whom I created for my glory, whom I formed and made."

Bring out the people who are blind,
yet have eyes, who are deaf, yet have ears!
All the nations gather together, and the peoples assemble.
Who among them can declare this,
and show us the former things?
Let them bring their witnesses to prove them right,
and let them hear and say, It is true.
"You are my witnesses," declares the Lord,
"and my servant whom I have chosen,
that you may know and believe me and understand that I am he.
Before me no god was formed, nor shall there be any after me.
I, I am the Lord, and besides me there is no savior.
I declared and saved and proclaimed,
when there was no strange god among you;
and you are my witnesses," declares the Lord, "and I am God."

Isaiah 43:1-12 ESV

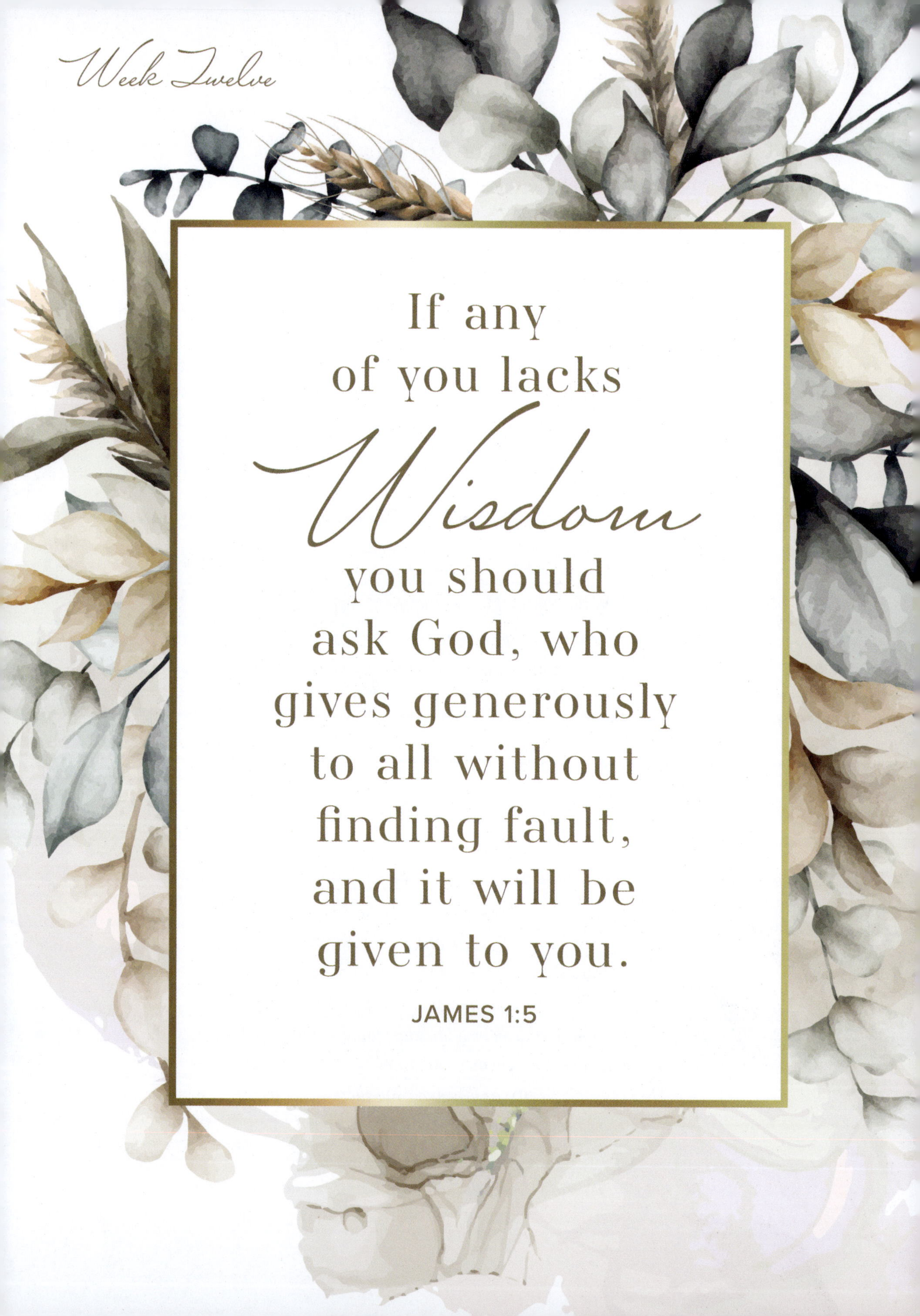
Week Twelve
If any
of you lacks
Wisdom
you should
ask God, who
gives generously
to all without
finding fault,
and it will be
given to you.
JAMES 1:5

Read

James 1:5–8

Remember

God promises to give generous wisdom when I ask for it.

Reflect

James 1:5 explains that God wants us to ask Him for wisdom. What promise supports this request? God gives wisdom generously, and He never negates our inabilities. He overflows with wisdom and guarantees it when we ask for it. Today's prayer promise is that God will abundantly reveal His wisdom when we humble ourselves. This promise is not a mere transaction of information but an intimate exchange where our humility becomes the fertile ground. God pours His divine wisdom. It's an assurance that God's response to our request for wisdom is not meager or reluctant but abundant and overflowing. His hand shapes our understanding and fosters a deeper connection with wisdom from above. Let's pray for it!

Father, give me Your wisdom from above.

Journal

Where do you need more wisdom in your life right now?

Pray

Praise

If any of you lacks wisdom,
let him ask God,
who gives generously to
all without reproach,
and it will be given him.
But let him ask in faith,
with no doubting,
for the one who doubts is like
a wave of the sea that is driven
and tossed by the wind.
For that person must not suppose that
he will receive anything from the Lord;
he is a double-minded man,
unstable in all his ways.

James 1:5-8 ESV

Week Thirteen
God is Light
IN HIM THERE IS NO DARKNESS AT ALL.
1 JOHN 1:5

Read

1 John 1:5–10

Remember

God promises fellowship when I walk in His light.

Reflect

John 1:5–10 assures us that we can live in the light, free from darkness. Confession plays a crucial role in enjoying fellowship with Jesus and other Christians. When we ask for forgiveness and repent, God forgives us and welcomes us. The light represents living within God's heavenly truth. When we pray this promise, we are asking God to forgive us and purify our hearts in love and truth. And when we fail and find ourselves asking for forgiveness again, remember God's promise of light and freedom is not a one-time transaction but a transformative journey. Embracing God's promise results in a continual renewal of our souls in the radiant light of His heavenly truth. Light for your journey is available through Jesus.

Father, forgive me and teach me to walk in the light.

Journal

Where in my life do I need to get honest before the Lord?

Pray

Praise

This is the message we have heard from
him and proclaim to you, that God is light,
and in him is no darkness at all.
If we say we have fellowship with him while we
walk in darkness, we lie and do not practice the truth.
But if we walk in the light, as he is in the light,
we have fellowship with one another,
and the blood of Jesus his Son
cleanses us from all sin. If we say we have no sin,
we deceive ourselves, and the truth is not in us.
If we confess our sins, he is faithful and
just to forgive us our sins and to cleanse us from
all unrighteousness. If we say we have not sinned,
we make him a liar, and his word is not in us.

1 John 1:5-10 ESV

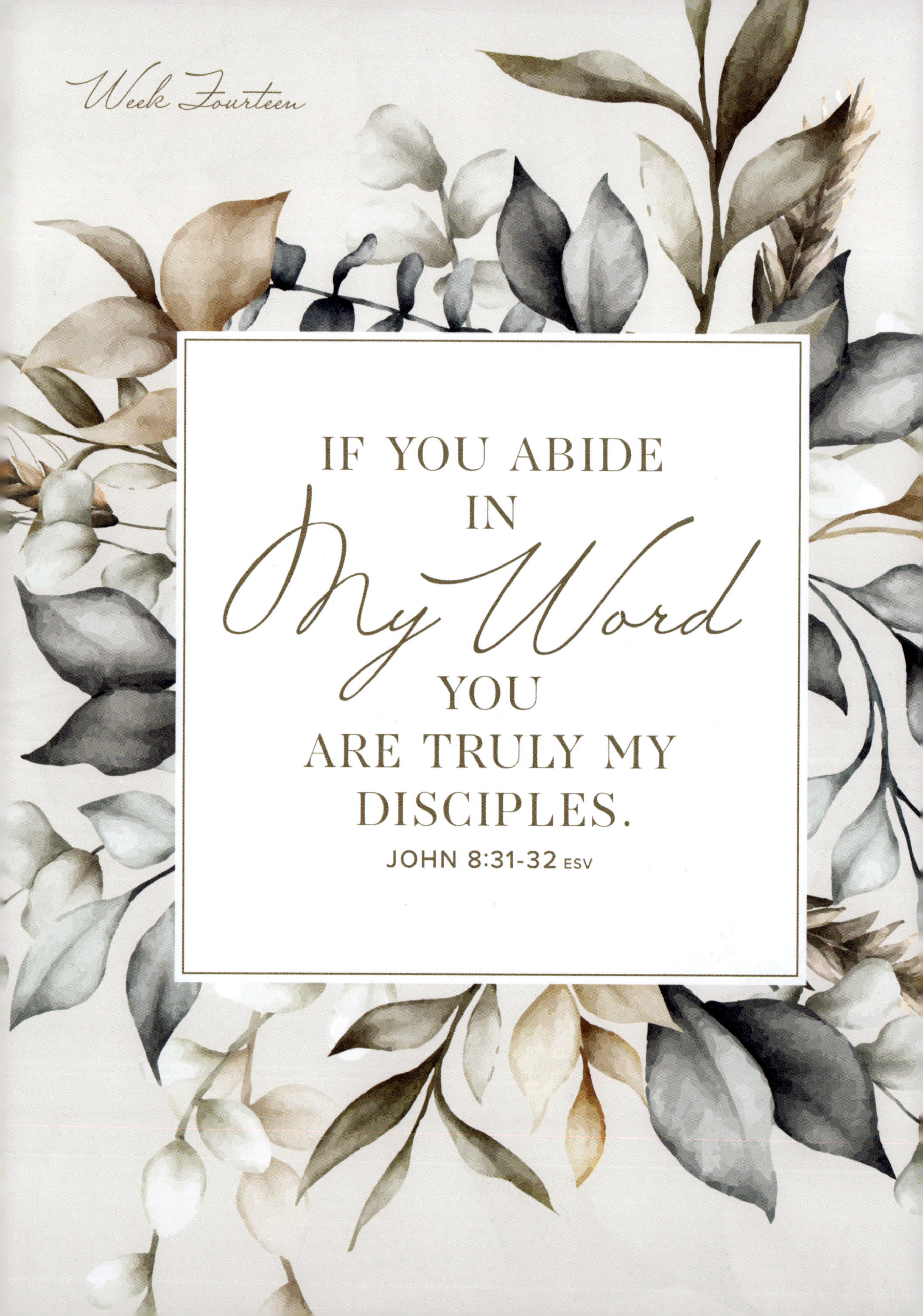
Week Fourteen
IF YOU ABIDE
IN
My Word
YOU
ARE TRULY MY
DISCIPLES.
JOHN 8:31-32 ESV

Read

John 8:30–46

Remember

God promises that the truth will set me free.

Reflect

The desire for freedom is born the moment a human being is born. We all long to experience freedom. But freedom for or from what? Most of the time, we think of freedom as being able to do our own thing when we want to. Or we label freedom as the ability to work and live according to our preferences. Jesus explains in John 8:30–46 that spiritual freedom comes when you hold to God's Word and His promises. If you know His promises, you understand the truth. Pure freedom is believing in God's promises and obeying His truths. It's a journey where belief in His promises becomes the compass guiding our choices, and obedience to His truths sets the spirit free. This freedom isn't just an individual experience; it ripples into our interactions with others, fostering a community marked by the power of God's promises.

Father, help me seek Your truth and obey it.

Journal

What is the relationship between knowing God's promises and having true freedom?

Pray

Praise

As he was saying these things, many believed in him.

So Jesus said to the Jews who had believed him, "If you abide in my word, you are truly my disciples, and you will know the truth, and the truth will set you free." They answered him, "We are offspring of Abraham and have never been enslaved to anyone. How is it that you say, 'You will become free'?"

Jesus answered them, "Truly, truly, I say to you, everyone who practices sin is a slave to sin. The slave does not remain in the house forever; the son remains forever. So if the Son sets you free, you will be free indeed. I know that you are offspring of Abraham; yet you seek to kill me because my word finds no place in you. I speak of what I have seen with my Father, and you do what you have heard from your father." They answered him, "Abraham is our father." Jesus said to them, "If you were Abraham's children, you would be doing the works Abraham did, but now you seek to kill me, a man who has told you the truth that I heard from God. This is not what Abraham did. You are doing the works your father did." They said to him, "We were not born of sexual immorality. We have one Father—even God." Jesus said to them, "If God were your Father, you would love me, for I came from God and I am here. I came not of my own accord, but he sent me. Why do you not understand what I say? It is because you cannot bear to hear my word. You are of your father the devil, and your will is to do your father's desires. He was a murderer from the beginning, and does not stand in the truth, because there is no truth in him. When he lies, he speaks out of his own character, for he is a liar and the father of lies. But because I tell the truth, you do not believe me. Which one of you convicts me of sin? If I tell the truth, why do you not believe me?

John 8:30-46 ESV

Week Fifteen

I THE LORD DO NOT *Change.*

MALACHI 3:6 ESV

Read

Malachi 3:6–12

Remember

God promises He will never change.

Reflect

The world is constantly changing, and just when you feel like you've settled into a routine, circumstances shift. In today's passage, the Lord speaks to His people through the prophet Malachi and boldly states: "I the *Lord* do not change." Even though the children of Israel have failed to tithe and keep His commandments, God has not destroyed them. Like us, God makes Himself available to His people and promises that if they return to Him, He will be there for them. He even challenges us to "test me in this" and vows to pour out so many blessings that there will not be enough room to hold them. Remember that God's love for you never changes.

Father, thank You for being the never-changing, loving God.

Journal

What has God done for me that reminds me of His bountiful blessings?

Pray

Praise

For I the LORD do not change; therefore you,
O children of Jacob, are not consumed.
From the days of your fathers you have turned
aside from my statutes and have not kept them.
Return to me, and I will return to you,
says the LORD of hosts. But you say,
"How shall we return?" Will man rob God?
Yet you are robbing me. But you say,
"How have we robbed you?"
In your tithes and contributions.
You are cursed with a curse, for you are robbing me,
the whole nation of you. Bring the full tithe into
the storehouse, that there may be food in my house.
And thereby put me to the test, says the LORD of hosts,
if I will not open the windows of heaven
for you and pour down for you a blessing until there
is no more need. I will rebuke the devourer for you,
so that it will not destroy the fruits of your soil,
and your vine in the field shall not
fail to bear, says the LORD of hosts.
Then all nations will call you blessed,
for you will be a land of delight,
says the LORD of hosts.

Malachi 3:6-12 ESV

Week Sixteen

THEREFORE
I TELL YOU,
whatever
you ask
IN
PRAYER,
BELIEVE THAT
YOU HAVE
RECIEVED IT,
AND IT WILL
BE YOURS.

MARK 11:24 ESV

Read

Mark 11:19–25

Remember

God promises to answer my prayers.

Reflect

In today's passage, Jesus speaks to Peter about a fig tree that He had commanded to wither due to its fruitlessness. When Peter saw that the fig tree had faded, he was surprised. Despite spending a lot of time with Jesus, Peter still had doubts. Jesus reminded Peter that the way to receive answered prayers is to ask in faith, believing God's promises. Jesus said, "Whatever you ask in prayer, believe that you have received it, and it will be yours." This prayer deepens your faith, expands your belief beyond your capabilities, and relies on God to be your all in all. Embrace it today!

Father, increase my faith to expand my requests according to Your promises.

Journal

What doubts need to be crossed out and replaced with "Believing God"?

Pray

Praise

And when evening came they went out of the city.

As they passed by in the morning,
they saw the fig tree withered away to its roots.
And Peter remembered and said to him,
"Rabbi, look! The fig tree that you cursed has withered."
And Jesus answered them, "Have faith in God.
Truly, I say to you, whoever says to this mountain,
'Be taken up and thrown into the sea,'
and does not doubt in his heart, but believes that
what he says will come to pass, it will be done for him.
Therefore I tell you, whatever you ask in prayer,
believe that you have received it, and it will be yours.
And whenever you stand praying, forgive,
if you have anything against anyone,
so that your Father also who is in heaven
may forgive you your trespasses."

Mark 11:19-25 ESV

Week Seventeen
MY GOD WILL
SUPPLY ALL
your needs
ACCORDING
TO HIS RICHES IN
GLORY IN
CHRIST JESUS.
PHILIPPIANS 4:19 NASB

Read

Philippians 4:10–20

Remember

God promises to meet all my needs.

Reflect

Every individual in the world has certain needs, whether they are physical, mental, emotional, or spiritual. However, you can find peace in the assurance that your God is more powerful than your needs. Your heavenly Father possesses an abundance of strength and resources beyond your comprehension. He will provide you with the strength you need in the required amount. Through Jesus, God will fulfill all of your needs according to His perfect redemptive plan. Like Paul, who understood the meaning of being in need, you can rely on Jesus for everything. You can trust His promises and depend on Him for heart contentment.

Father, may my desires and needs match what You have for me.

Journal

How can you trust in God's promises and lean on Him to provide for your every need, just like Paul did?

Pray

Praise

But I rejoiced in the Lord greatly, that now at last you have revived your concern for me; indeed, you were concerned before, but you lacked an opportunity to act. Not that I speak from need, for I have learned to be content in whatever circumstances I am. I know how to get along with little, and I also know how to live in prosperity; in any and every circumstance I have learned the secret of being filled and going hungry, both of having abundance and suffering need. I can do all things through Him who strengthens me. Nevertheless, you have done well to share with me in my difficulty.

You yourselves also know, Philippians, that at the first preaching of the gospel, after I left Macedonia, no church shared with me in the matter of giving and receiving except you alone; for even in Thessalonica you sent a gift more than once for my needs. Not that I seek the gift itself, but I seek the profit which increases to your account. But I have received everything in full and have an abundance; I am amply supplied, having received from Epaphroditus what you have sent, a fragrant aroma, an acceptable sacrifice, pleasing to God. And my God will supply all your needs according to His riches in glory in Christ Jesus. Now to our God and Father be the glory forever and ever. Amen.

Philippians 4:10-20 NASB

Week Eighteen
Delight yourself
in
the LORD, and He
will give you
the desires
of your heart.
PSALM 37:4 ESV

Read

Psalm 37:1–6

Remember

God promises to fulfill me when I delight in Him.

Reflect

Psalm 37 is full of promises that require our cooperation. Although God doesn't need our help to fulfill His promises, He wants us to trust that He is always ready and willing to work on our behalf. This means we must be prepared and willing to work with Him. Putting our trust in His promises is wise because our commitment level changes for the better. When we give ourselves entirely to Him, our desires align with His, and we receive unparalleled blessings. This is the promise God offers to those who rely on Him—that's you!

Father, make my delight to be in only You.

Journal

What does it mean to me to "take delight in the Lord"?

Pray

Praise

Fret not yourself because of evildoers;
be not envious of wrongdoers!
For they will soon fade like the grass
and wither like the green herb.

Trust in the L*ORD*, *and do good;*
dwell in the land and befriend faithfulness.
Delight yourself in the L*ORD*,
and he will give you the desires of your heart.

Commit your way to the L*ORD*;
trust in him, and he will act.
He will bring forth your righteousness as the light,
and your justice as the noonday.

Psalm 37:1-6 ESV

Do not lean on your
own understanding.
In all your ways
Acknowledge
Him
and He will make
straight your paths.

PROVERBS 3:5-6 ESV

Read

Proverbs 3:5–8

Remember

God promises guidance when I rely on Him.

Reflect

Have you ever struggled to let go of your ideas or opinions? Whether due to habit or stubbornness, we often find it hard to abandon our beliefs. Proverbs 3:5 advises us not to rely solely on our understanding. The Amplified version of the verse emphasizes this by stating, "Do not rely on your own insight." Surrender is the key to receiving God's promises of clear direction, guidance, and opportunity. It's natural to want to stick to our ways because we like to think logically. But when we trust God, He promises us clear direction, guidance, and opportunity. You can trust God completely, and by doing so, you will honor and come to understand His Word.

Father, bolster my heart to trust in You.

Journal

Where am I tempted to trust my judgment more than rely on God?

Pray

Praise

Trust in and rely confidently
on the Lord with all your heart
And do not rely on your
own insight or understanding.

In all your ways know and
acknowledge and recognize Him,
And He will make your paths straight and smooth
[removing obstacles that block your way].

Do not be wise in your own eyes;
Fear the Lord [with reverent awe and obedience]
and turn [entirely] away from evil.

It will be health to your body
[your marrow, your nerves, your sinews,
your muscles—all your inner parts]
And refreshment (physical well-being)
to your bones.

Proverbs 3:5-8 AMP

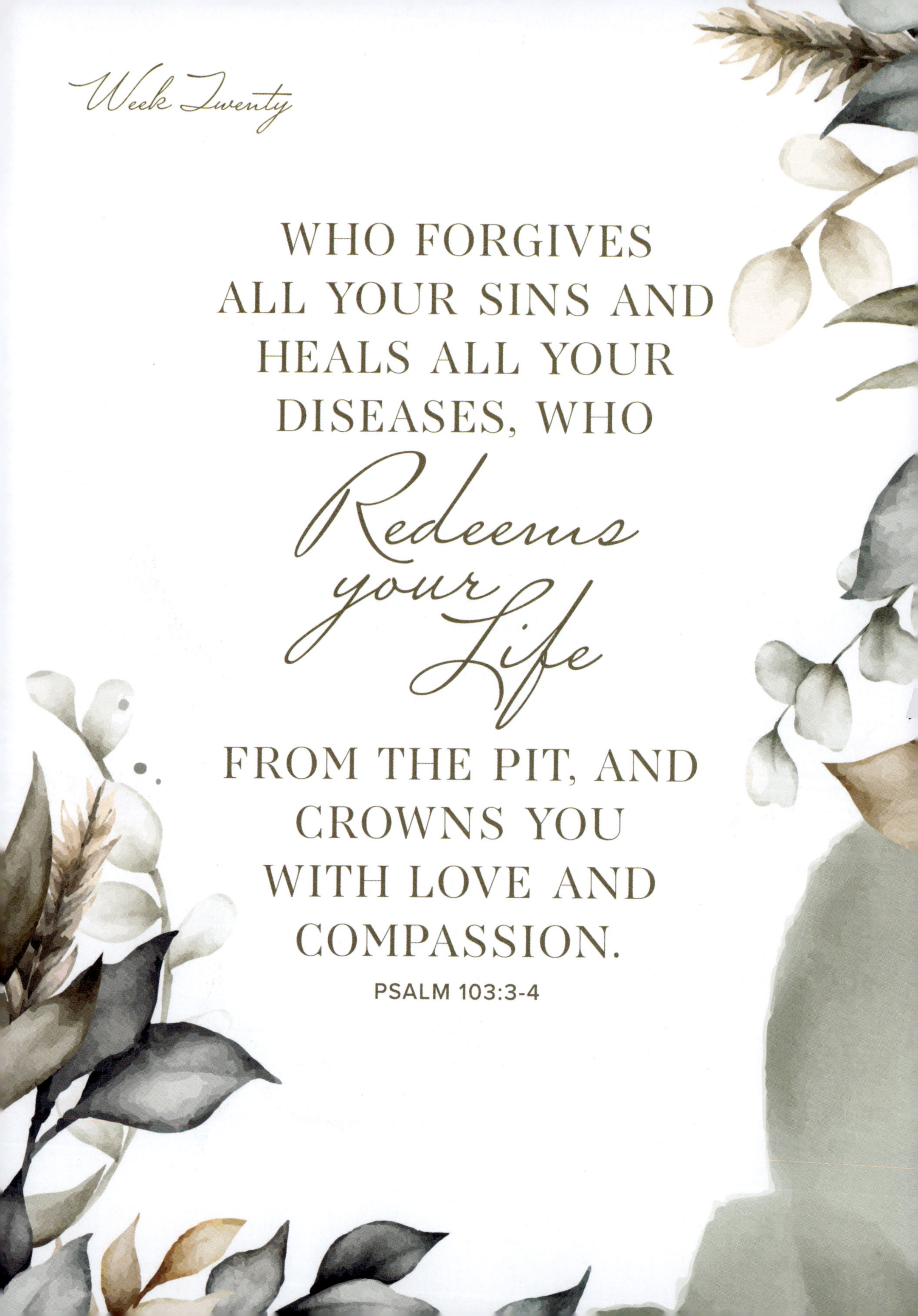

Week Twenty

WHO FORGIVES
ALL YOUR SINS AND
HEALS ALL YOUR
DISEASES, WHO
Redeems
your
Life
FROM THE PIT, AND
CROWNS YOU
WITH LOVE AND
COMPASSION.

PSALM 103:3-4

Read

Psalm 103:1–5

Remember

God promises to redeem my life from the pit.

Reflect

Our God is merciful and forgiving; He heals and loves us with compassion, and satisfies our desires with good things. He restores our bodies, minds, and spirits. The promise of what God can do for us is immeasurable. David knew this and, in today's key verse, he praises the Lord, witnessing God's work of forgiveness in his own life. It's worth noting that the lyrics were written as a testimony of past events and an account of present experiences. Our God's devotion to His creation is beyond measure, but it should be remembered.

Father, bring to my memory all You've done for me.

Journal

What are some good things that God has blessed you with, and how have you seen His restoration in your body, mind, and spirit?

Pray

Praise

Bless the Lord, O my soul,
and all that is within me,
bless his holy name!
Bless the Lord, O my soul,
and forget not all his benefits,
who forgives all your iniquity,
who heals all your diseases,
who redeems your life from the pit,
who crowns you with steadfast love and mercy,
who satisfies you with good so that
your youth is renewed like the eagle's.

Psalm 103:1-5 ESV

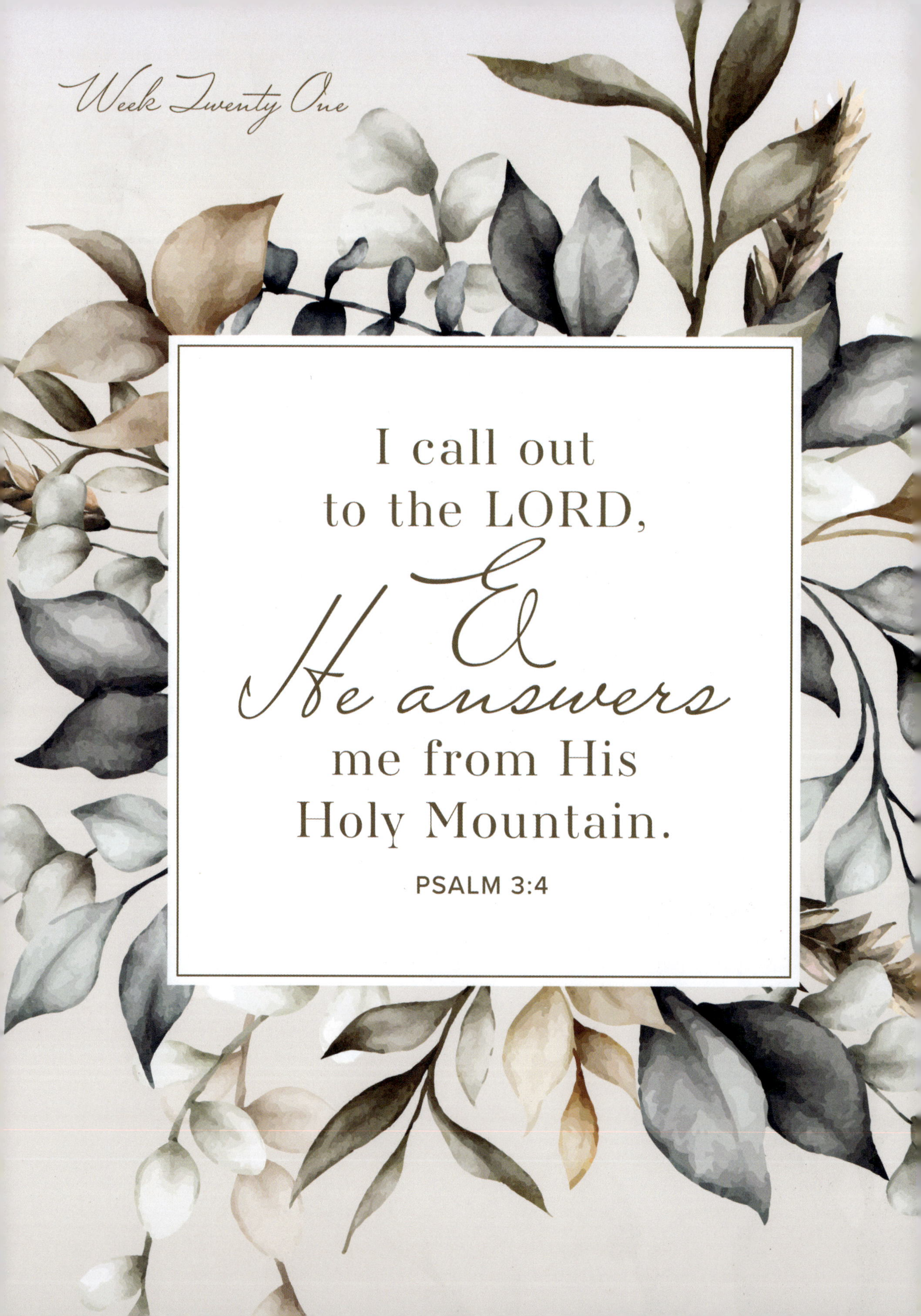
Week Twenty One
I call out
to the LORD,
&
He answers
me from His
Holy Mountain.
PSALM 3:4

Read

Psalm 3:1–8

Remember

God promises to answer when I call out to Him.

Reflect

In moments of distress, it's natural to seek a quick solution or reach out to a friend for support. While there's nothing wrong with seeking help from trustworthy people around us, God is ever-present and listens for the cries of our hearts. Making prayer our first response to struggles reveals how we prioritize prayer. Make no mistake, your heavenly Father leans in to hear your heart beating in prayer. In today's passage, David's example is a powerful reminder that even in the darkest nights, we can find solace in prayer and our Creator's presence. In moments of fear or doubt, your God is nearer than the enemy who surrounds you.

Father, prompt me to pray at the first sign of trouble.

Journal

How can you make prayer your response to the "first sign of struggle" today?

Pray

Praise

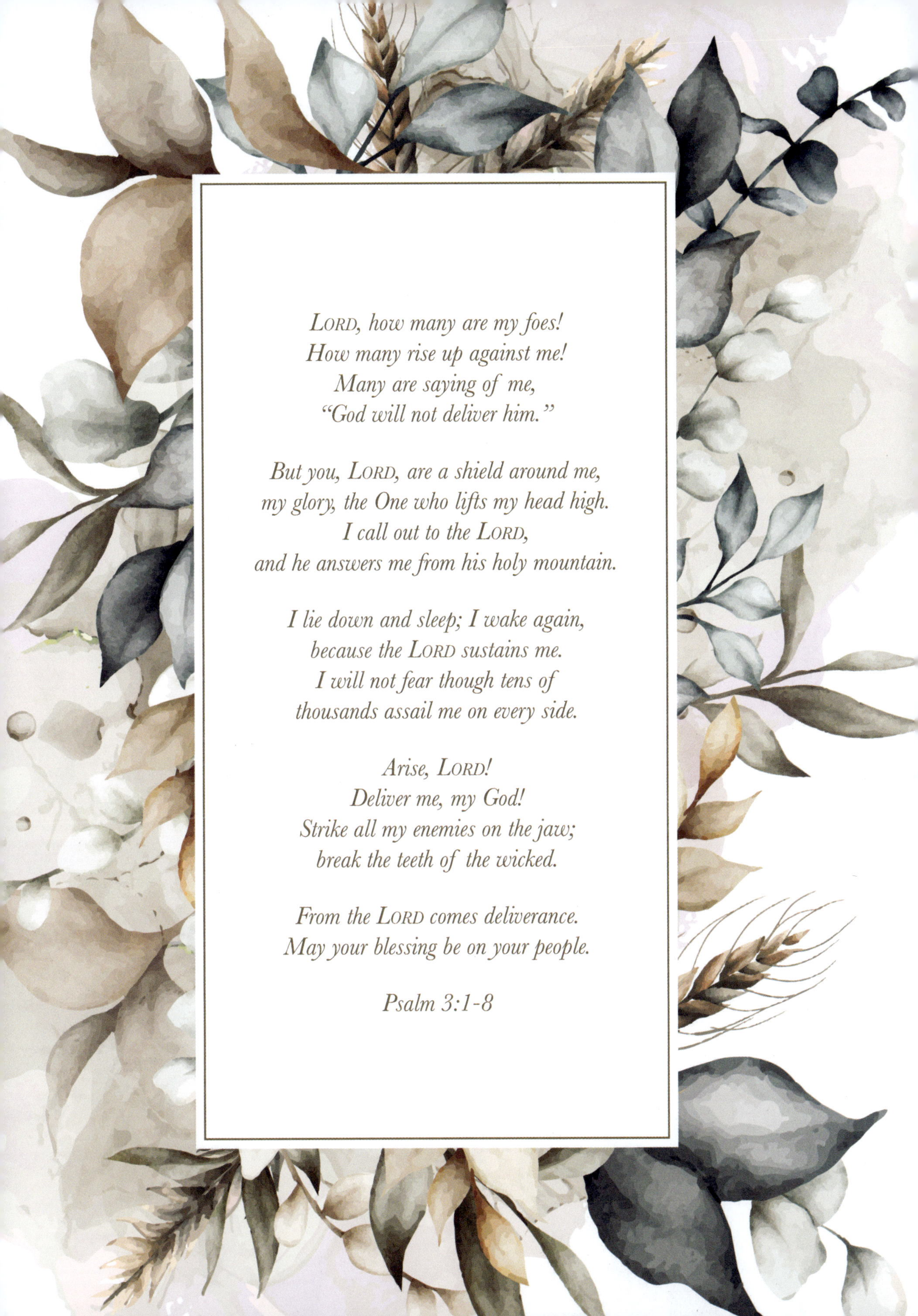

Lord, how many are my foes!
How many rise up against me!
Many are saying of me,
"God will not deliver him."

But you, Lord, are a shield around me,
my glory, the One who lifts my head high.
I call out to the Lord,
and he answers me from his holy mountain.

I lie down and sleep; I wake again,
because the Lord sustains me.
I will not fear though tens of
thousands assail me on every side.

Arise, Lord!
Deliver me, my God!
Strike all my enemies on the jaw;
break the teeth of the wicked.

From the Lord comes deliverance.
May your blessing be on your people.

Psalm 3:1-8

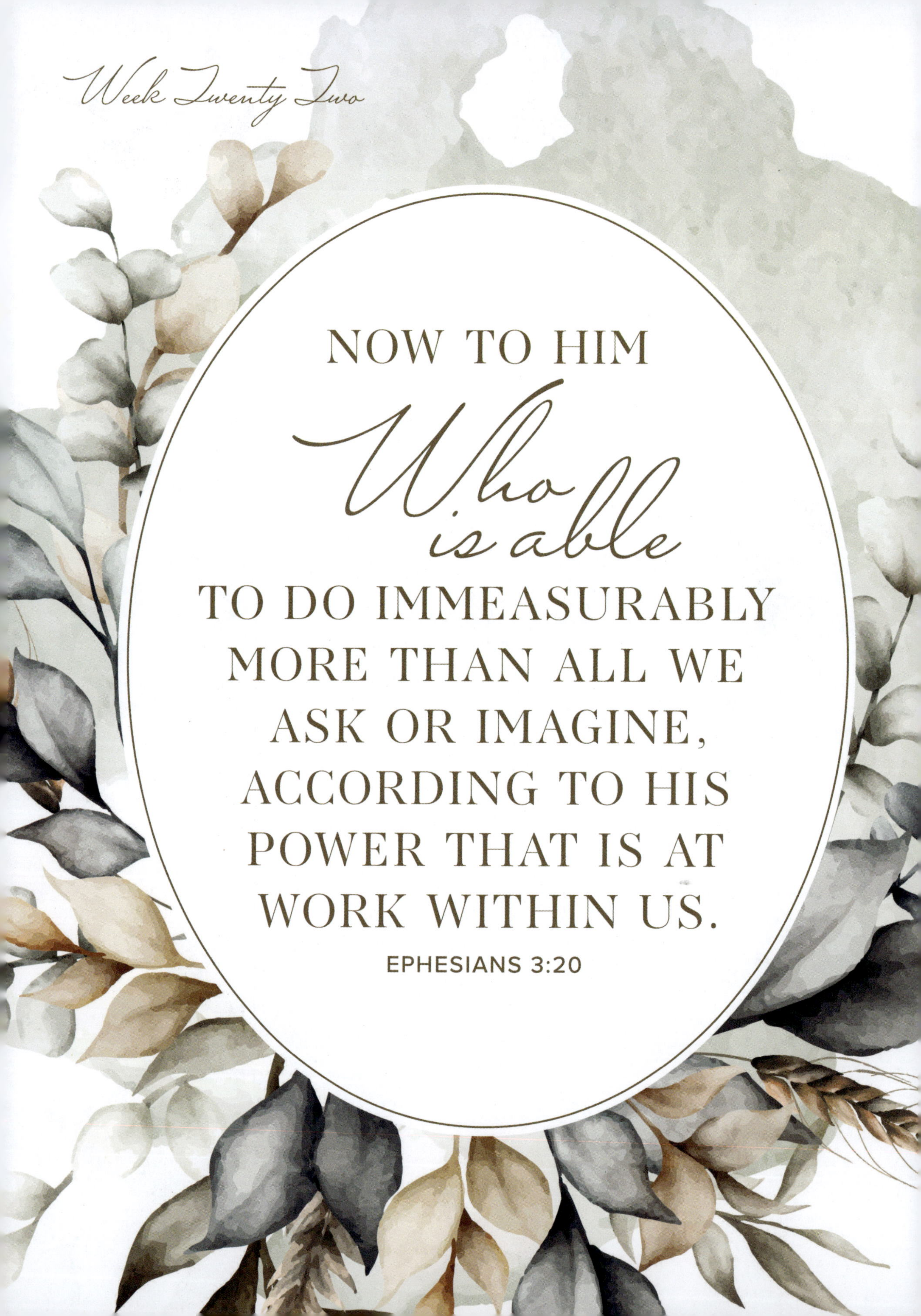
Week Twenty Two
NOW TO HIM
Who
is able
TO DO IMMEASURABLY
MORE THAN ALL WE
ASK OR IMAGINE,
ACCORDING TO HIS
POWER THAT IS AT
WORK WITHIN US.
EPHESIANS 3:20

Read

Ephesians 3:16–20

Remember

God promises to do more than I can ask or imagine.

Reflect

Have you ever wondered what the moment will be like when Jesus returns? In today's key passage, the apostle Paul provides us with a glimpse into some of the details of that coming day. However, the most awe-inspiring detail about this event is that death will be conquered and swallowed up in victory. Jesus' triumph over the cross and death guarantees salvation to all who believe in Him. We can confidently stand firm in our faith, knowing that our work in the Lord is steadfast and never in vain. When all seems lost or uncertain, when the winds of this world blow wildly, know that your work in the Lord is sure, never in vain.

Father, thank You for doing more than I can ever imagine.

Journal

How does the assurance of salvation impact how I view my daily work?

Pray

Praise

I pray that out of his glorious riches he may strengthen
you with power through his Spirit in your inner being,
so that Christ may dwell in your hearts through faith.
And I pray that you, being rooted and established in love,
may have power, together with all the Lord's holy people,
to grasp how wide and long and high and deep is the love of Christ,
and to know this love that surpasses knowledge—that you
may be filled to the measure of all the fullness of God.

Now to him who is able to do immeasurably
more than all we ask or imagine,
according to his power that is at work within us.

Ephesians 3:16-20

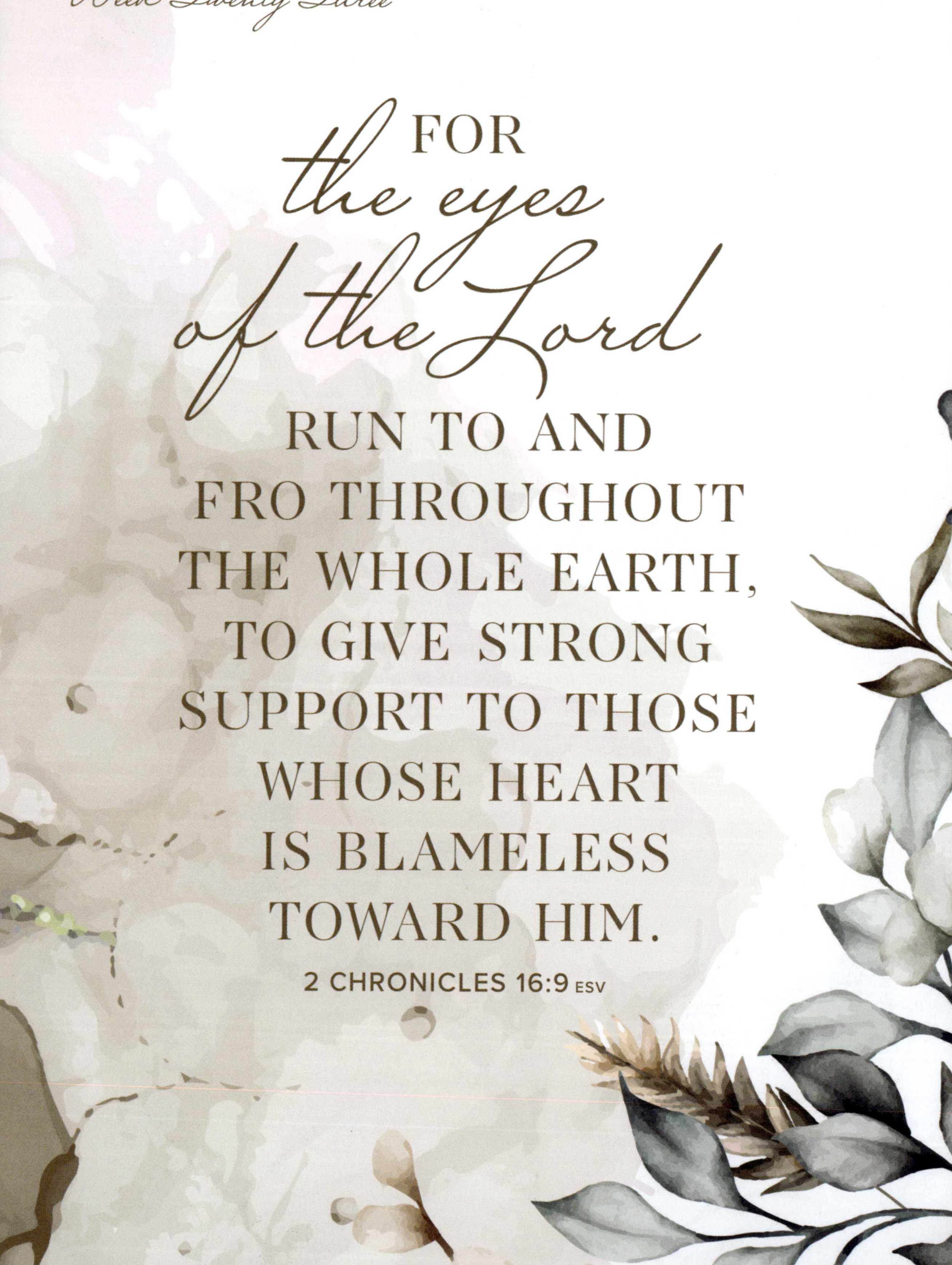
Week Twenty Three
FOR
the eyes
of the Lord
RUN TO AND
FRO THROUGHOUT
THE WHOLE EARTH,
TO GIVE STRONG
SUPPORT TO THOSE
WHOSE HEART
IS BLAMELESS
TOWARD HIM.
2 CHRONICLES 16:9 ESV

Read

2 Chronicles 16:7–9

Remember

God promises to honor those with fully committed hearts.

Reflect

Have you ever observed parents training their children to walk beside them while they stroll in a grocery store? They may not be holding their child's hand, but their gaze hardly leaves the child. Each parent's top priority is to ensure proximity and safety. This is similar to our relationship with our heavenly Father. He desires to keep us close to His heart so He can protect and secure us from harm. We receive His closest assistance when we remain near to Him. He has promised to honor your commitment to Him. Are you doing the same?

Father, let the state of my heart be pleasing to You.

Journal

Have you ever lost something and then found it? How do those feelings apply to today's promise?

Pray

Praise

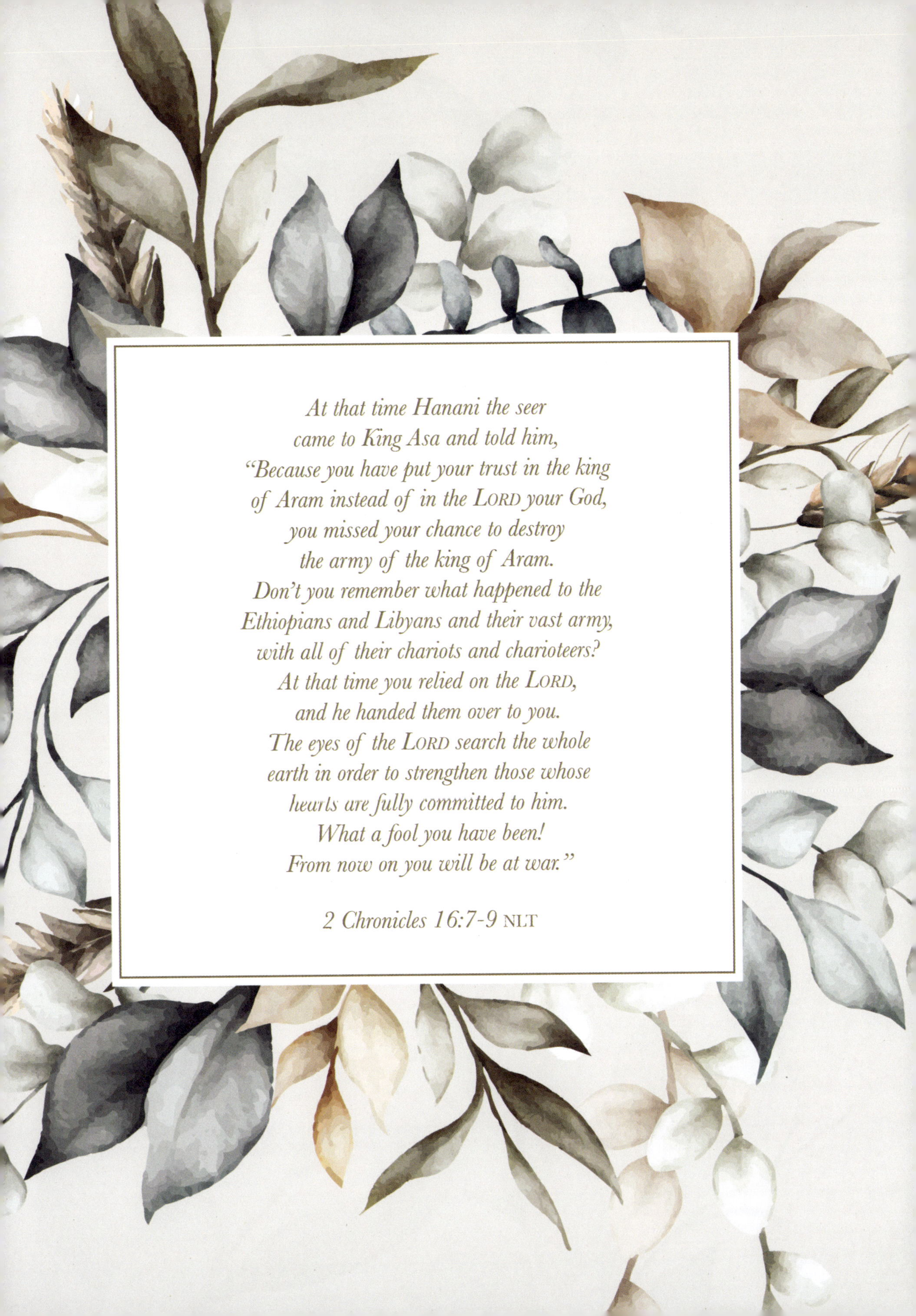

At that time Hanani the seer
came to King Asa and told him,
"Because you have put your trust in the king
of Aram instead of in the LORD *your God,*
you missed your chance to destroy
the army of the king of Aram.
Don't you remember what happened to the
Ethiopians and Libyans and their vast army,
with all of their chariots and charioteers?
At that time you relied on the LORD,
and he handed them over to you.
The eyes of the LORD *search the whole*
earth in order to strengthen those whose
hearts are fully committed to him.
What a fool you have been!
From now on you will be at war."

2 Chronicles 16:7-9 NLT

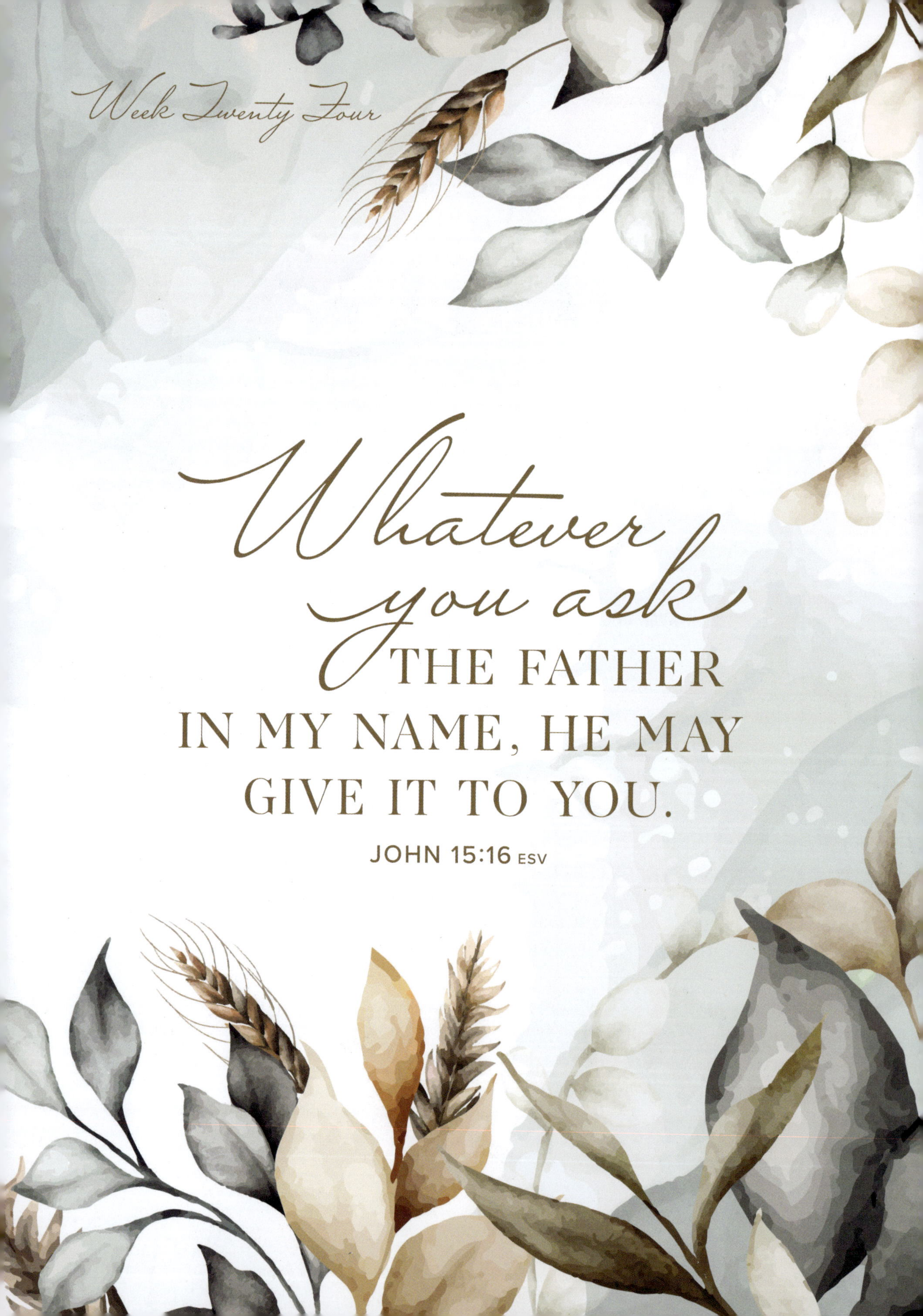
Week Twenty Four
Whatever
you ask
THE FATHER
IN MY NAME, HE MAY
GIVE IT TO YOU.
JOHN 15:16 ESV

Read

John 15:12–17

Remember

God promises I will see fruit when I love others.

Reflect

As we've already seen, God sometimes pairs a command with a promise. These statements often begin with "if we …" and are followed by "then He…." In John 15, Jesus says that if we obey Him and bear fruit of that following, whatever we ask in Jesus' name, the Father will give to us. However, it all begins with loving God and others. It may seem like a straightforward concept, but in reality, to genuinely love people requires God's love flowing through us. When we're tapped into God's strength, serving and loving others selflessly becomes effortless. When we strive to abide in Christ and bear fruit that glorifies Him, we position ourselves to receive God's promises. Who needs God's love in your circle of influence today?

Father, help me to be the friend I need.

Journal

What does bearing fruit look like right now in my life?

Pray

Praise

*This is my commandment:
Love each other in the same
way I have loved you.
There is no greater love than to
lay down one's life for one's friends.
You are my friends if you do what
I command. I no longer call you slaves,
because a master doesn't confide in his slaves.
Now you are my friends, since I have told
you everything the Father told me.
You didn't choose me. I chose you.
I appointed you to go and
produce lasting fruit, so that
the Father will give you whatever
you ask for, using my name.
This is my command: Love each other.*

John 15:12-17 NLT

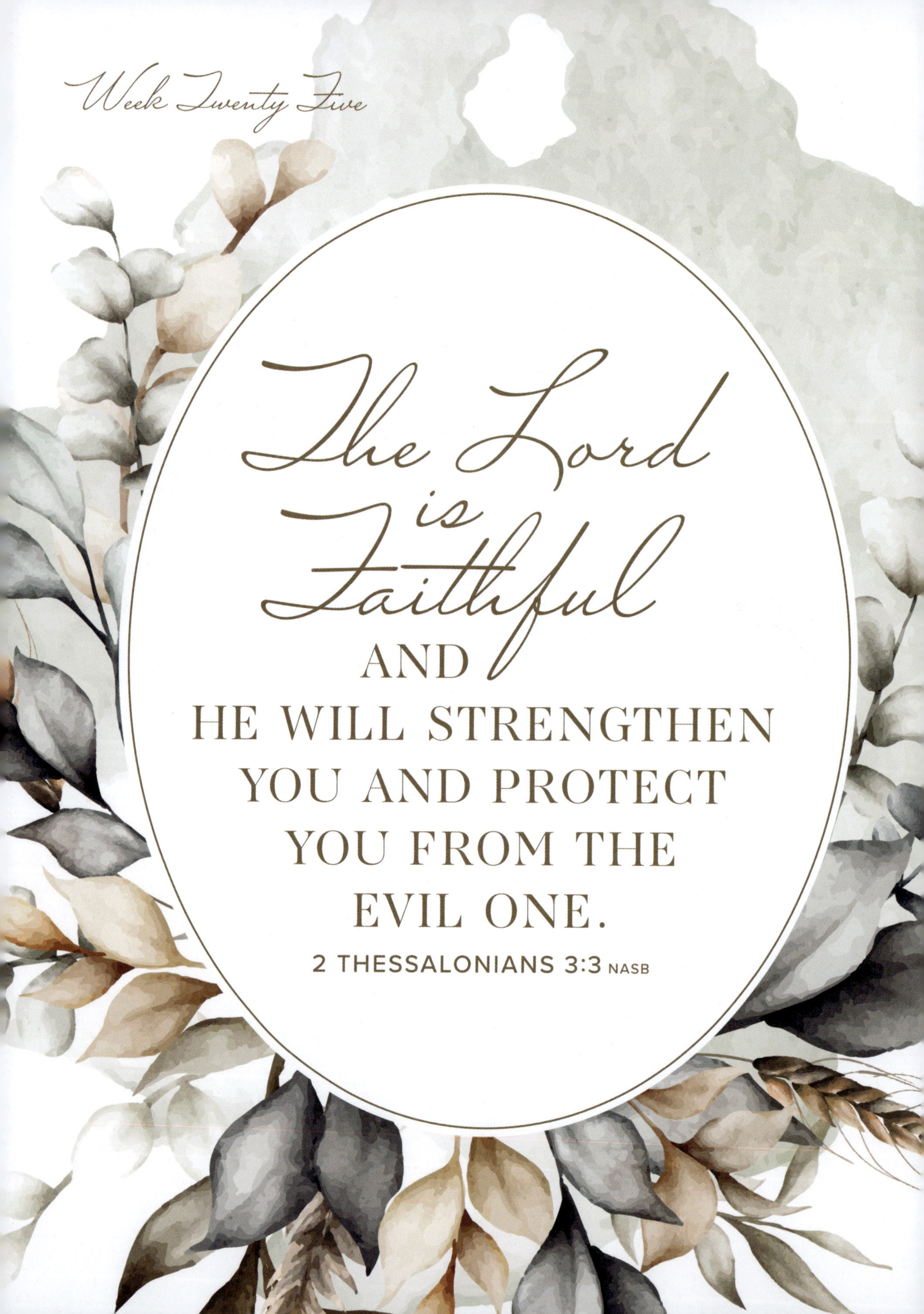
Week Twenty Five
The Lord is Faithful
AND
HE WILL STRENGTHEN
YOU AND PROTECT
YOU FROM THE
EVIL ONE.
2 THESSALONIANS 3:3 NASB

Read

2 Thessalonians 3:1–5

Remember

God promises to be your power and preservation.

Reflect

Paul is writing to the Thessalonian church, asking them to pray for his team. But after two lines of requesting prayer, he offers a statement that should arrest our attention. "But the Lord is faithful, and He will strengthen and protect you from the evil one" (NASB). It doesn't matter what comes before the "but," though many are faithless and the enemy is raging, our God is faithful and protective. He faithfully provides the strength you need and He guards your heart.

Father, grant me Your perseverance and keep me from falling.

Journal

Where do I need the reminder that the Lord is faithful?

Pray

Praise

Finally, brothers and sisters,
pray for us that the word of the Lord
will spread rapidly and be glorified,
just as it was also with you;
and that we will be rescued from
troublesome and evil people;
for not all have the faith.
But the Lord is faithful,
and He will strengthen and protect
you from the evil one.
We have confidence in the Lord
concerning you, that you are doing,
and will do, what we command.
May the Lord direct your hearts to the love
of God and to the perseverance of Christ.

2 Thessalonians 3:1-5 NASB

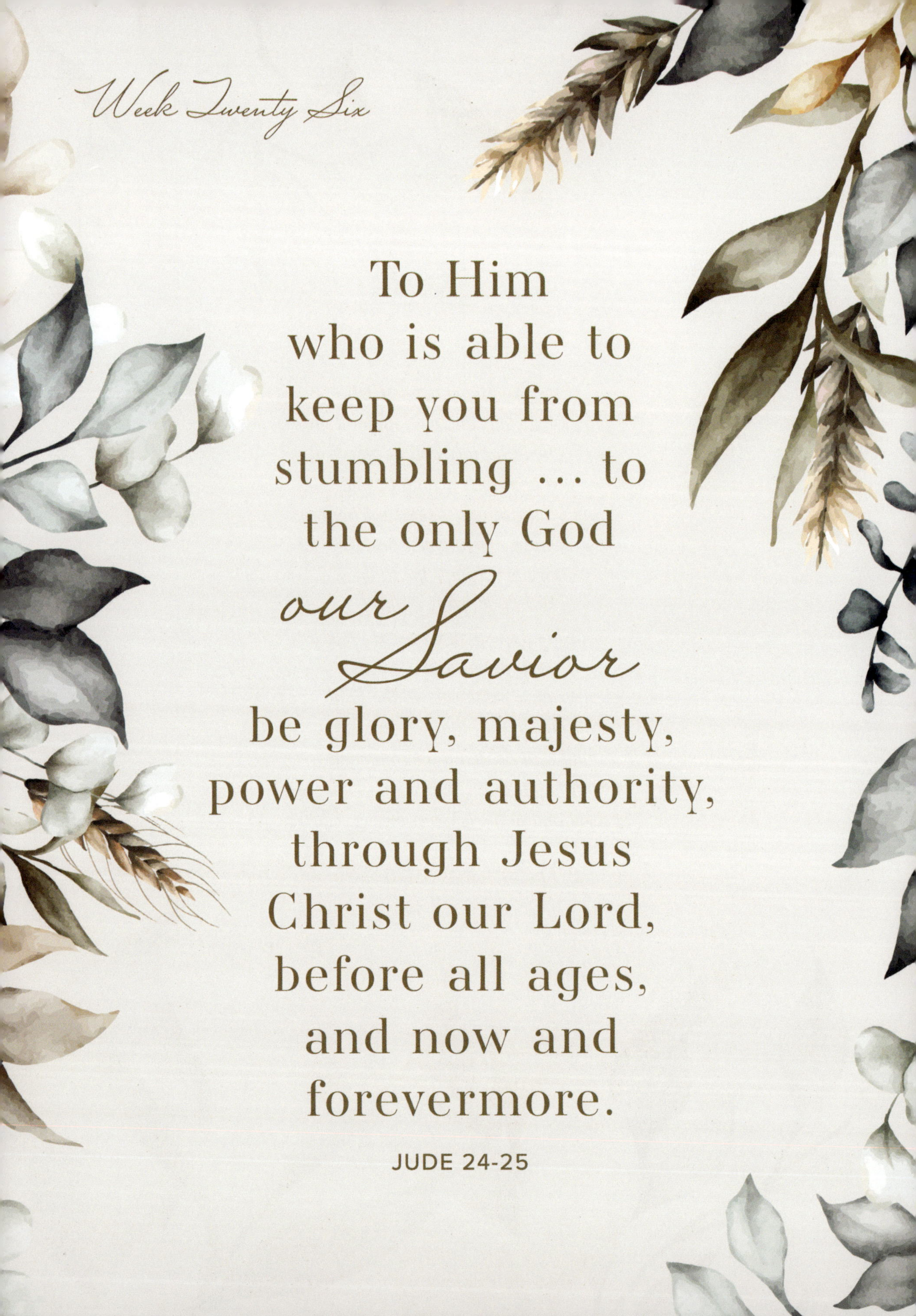

Week Twenty Six

To Him
who is able to
keep you from
stumbling ... to
the only God
our Savior
be glory, majesty,
power and authority,
through Jesus
Christ our Lord,
before all ages,
and now and
forevermore.

JUDE 24-25

Read

Ephesians 3:14–21

Remember

God promises to keep me from stumbling.

Reflect

The book of Jude is a powerful reminder to hold on to our faith, even amid adversity. This short yet impactful single-chapter book in the Bible inspires us to stay steadfast in our belief. Today's key verse is a doxology, a form of praise combined with a promise. Let us exalt the Lord who owns glory, majesty, power, and authority! Hallelujah! Ephesians 3 also has a great doxology. Take a look at it below. Remember, Jesus is our rock, and He ensures that we do not falter in our faith. Jesus makes us perfect and then lovingly presents us to the Father. So, no matter our challenges, we can hold on to our faith and trust in the Lord. He will guide you through every storm; He promises!

Father, I look forward to spending time with You now and in the future.

Journal

What are three ways I can hold on to my faith in this season?

Pray

Praise

For this reason I kneel before the Father, from whom every family in heaven and on earth derives its name. I pray that out of his glorious riches he may strengthen you with power through his Spirit in your inner being, so that Christ may dwell in your hearts through faith. And I pray that you, being rooted and established in love, may have power, together with all the Lord's holy people, to grasp how wide and long and high and deep is the love of Christ, and to know this love that surpasses knowledge—that you may be filled to the measure of all the fullness of God.

Now to him who is able to do immeasurably more than all we ask or imagine, according to his power that is at work within us, to him be glory in the church and in Christ Jesus throughout all generations, for ever and ever! Amen.

Ephesians 3:14-21

Week Twenty Seven

"I AM *the Bread of Life*

WHOEVER COMES TO ME SHALL NOT HUNGER, AND WHOEVER BELIEVES IN ME SHALL NEVER THIRST."

JOHN 6:35 ESV

Read

John 6:35–40

Remember

God promises to be my daily bread.

Reflect

In the Gospel of John, Jesus proclaims, "I am the bread of life." This statement is truly captivating. According to Jesus, those who come to Him will never be hungry, and whoever believes in Him will never be thirsty. He doesn't mean this in a literal, physical sense. Because Jesus is our bread of life, the deep-seated yearning we all have can only be completely fulfilled by Jesus, our daily bread. He is our source of spiritual and emotional nourishment and sustenance and will be our portion forever. Every longing of your heart is fulfilled through Him because He is genuinely all you need.

Father, I trust Your promise of fulfillment in Christ.

Journal

What empty spaces of my heart crave a fresh filling from Jesus?

Pray

Praise

Jesus said to them, "I am the bread of life;
whoever comes to me shall not hunger,
and whoever believes in me shall never thirst.
But I said to you that you have seen me and yet do not believe.
All that the Father gives me will come to me,
and whoever comes to me I will never cast out.
For I have come down from heaven,
not to do my own will but the will of him who sent me.
And this is the will of him who sent me,
that I should lose nothing of all that he has given me,
but raise it up on the last day.
For this is the will of my Father,
that everyone who looks on the Son
and believes in him should have eternal life,
and I will raise him up on the last day."

John 6:35-40 ESV

Week Twenty-Eight

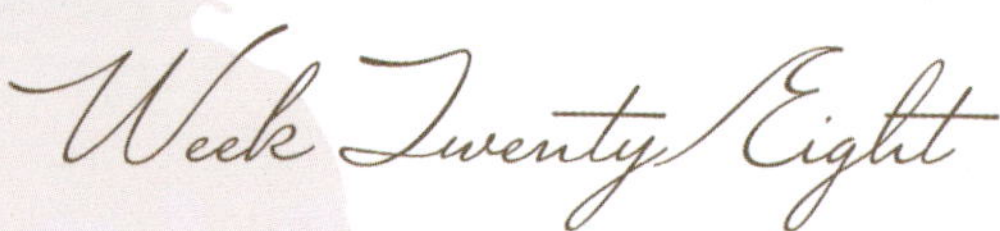

Then you
will call,
and
The Lord
will answer
You will cry
for help, and
He will say,
"Here I am."

ISAIAH 58:9 NASB

Read

Isaiah 58:3–12

Remember

God promises to answer my prayers when I cry for help.

Reflect

Do you feel like your prayers are going unanswered? Remember that God has promised to answer our prayers when we cry for help. His "here I am" reply is not a surprise, but a sign of affirmation. It's a reminder that God has been with us all along the way, even when we couldn't see Him working. We are His miracle. He created us, and we belong to Him. We don't have to know everything about the future. All we need to do is trust that He works everything out for our good, and then obey His Word and His Spirit. Here He is, with you always.

Father, help me to remember You always answer when I pray.

Journal

What is my response when my prayers go unanswered?

Pray

Praise

"Why have we fasted and You do not see?
Why have we humbled ourselves and You do not notice?"

Behold, on the day of your fast you find your desire, and oppress all your workers.
Behold, you fast for contention and strife, and to strike with a wicked fist.
You do not fast like you have done today to make your voice heard on high!
Is it a fast like this that I choose, a day for a person to humble himself?
Is it for bowing one's head like a reed and for spreading out sackcloth and
ashes as a bed? Will you call this a fast, even an acceptable day to the LORD?

Is this not the fast that I choose: to release the bonds of wickedness,
to undo the ropes of the yoke, and to let the oppressed go free,
and break every yoke? Is it not to break your bread with the hungry
and bring the homeless poor into the house; when you see the naked,
to cover him; and not to hide yourself from your own flesh?
Then your light will break out like the dawn, and your recovery
will spring up quickly; and your righteousness will go before you;
the glory of the LORD will be your rear guard. Then you will call,
and the LORD will answer; you will cry for help, and He will say, "Here I am."

If you remove the yoke from your midst, the pointing of the finger
and speaking wickedness, and if you offer yourself to the hungry
and satisfy the need of the afflicted, then your light will rise in darkness,
and your gloom will become like midday. And the LORD will continually guide you.
And satisfy your desire in scorched places, and give strength to your bones;
and you will be like a watered garden, and like a spring of water whose
waters do not fail. Those from among you will rebuild the ancient ruins;
you will raise up the age-old foundations; and you will be called
the repairer of the breach, the restorer of the streets in which to dwell.

Isaiah 58:3-12 NASB

Week Twenty Nine
THE
LORD IS
Trustworthy
IN ALL HE
PROMISES AND
FAITHFUL IN
ALL HE DOES.
PSALM 145:13

Read

Psalm 145:13–16

Remember

God promises to be trustworthy in all He promises.

Reflect

Humans are born with innate desires that guide us toward finding meaning and purpose in life. These desires include the yearning to be loved and known and living a fulfilling life. However, we often overlook that these desires were instilled in us by our Creator, who desires to fulfill all our needs. "[He opens His] hand and satisfies the desires of every living thing." We can trust that the Lord will faithfully fulfill all His promises and meet all our needs. While we may have questions, we can take comfort in knowing that our Creator has a good plan for our lives. You can trust that He will always provide His best for you.

Father, help me to focus on Your faithfulness.

Journal

How can I align my desires and purpose with my Creator's plan for my life?

Pray

Praise

Your kingdom is an everlasting kingdom,
and your dominion endures
through all generations.

The Lord is trustworthy in all he
promises and faithful in all he does.
The Lord upholds all who fall
and lifts up all who are bowed down.
The eyes of all look to you, and you
give them their food at the proper time.
You open your hand and satisfy
the desires of every living thing.

Psalm 145:13-16

Week Thirty
THE
LORD IS GOOD,
a Refuge
IN TIMES OF
TROUBLE.
NAHUM 1:7

Read

Nahum 1:3–7

Remember

God promises to care for me.

Reflect

Feeling nurtured is a great feeling for us as humans. God is good. He is a stronghold when we're distressed. But He is not a cold rock. The second part of today's key verse holds a nugget of truth that helps us want to trust God more. When we choose to trust Him, He nurtures that trust. He cultivates it, He waters it, and He nourishes it. So learning to trust God is not all our responsibility! We can rest in His power and goodness to nourish our choice of trusting Him. God will take care of you.

Father, help me recognize that You care for me and build my trust.

Journal

How does knowing that the Lord is trustworthy strengthen my heart?

Pray

Praise

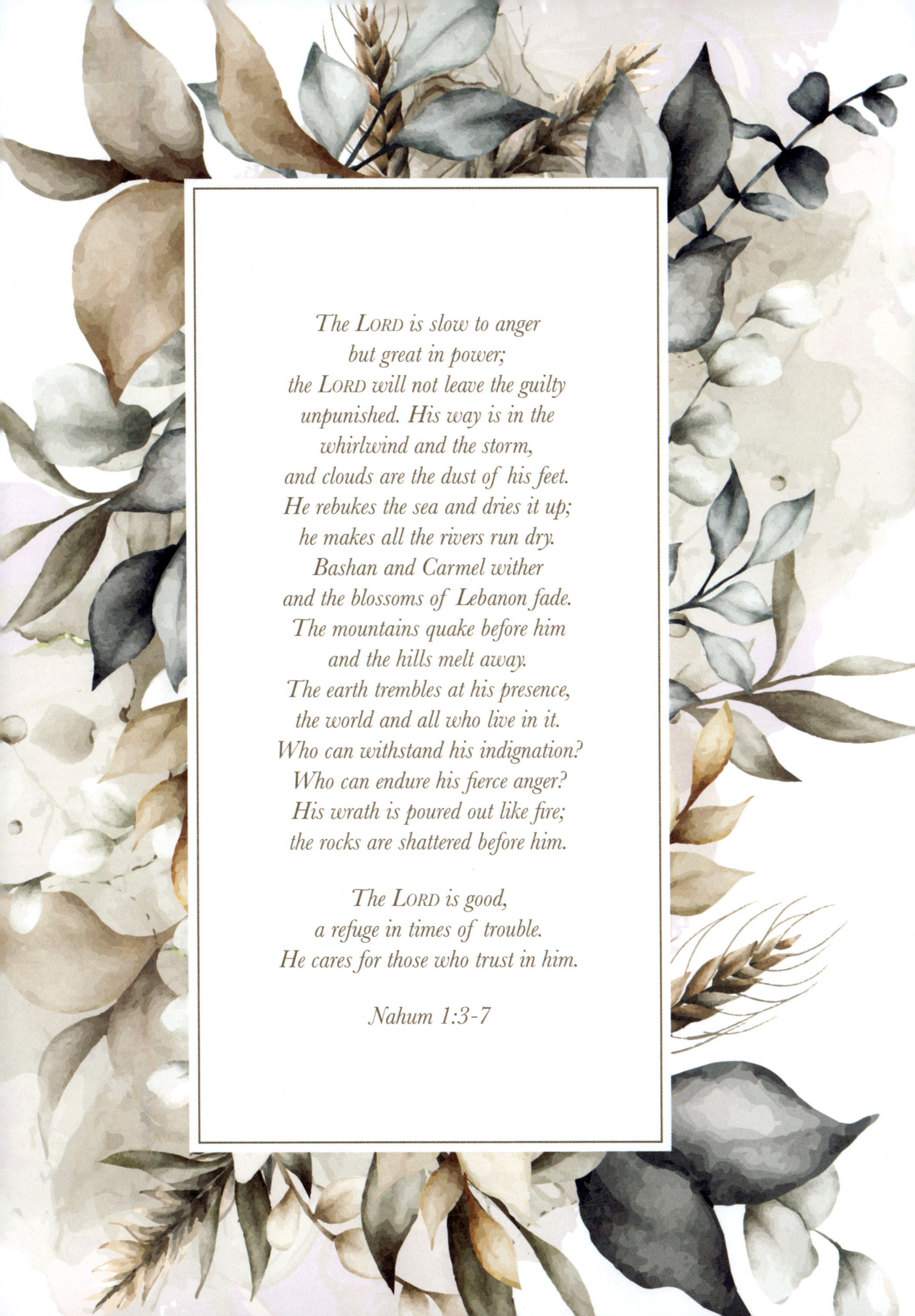

The LORD is slow to anger
but great in power;
the LORD will not leave the guilty
unpunished. His way is in the
whirlwind and the storm,
and clouds are the dust of his feet.
He rebukes the sea and dries it up;
he makes all the rivers run dry.
Bashan and Carmel wither
and the blossoms of Lebanon fade.
The mountains quake before him
and the hills melt away.
The earth trembles at his presence,
the world and all who live in it.
Who can withstand his indignation?
Who can endure his fierce anger?
His wrath is poured out like fire;
the rocks are shattered before him.

The LORD is good,
a refuge in times of trouble.
He cares for those who trust in him.

Nahum 1:3-7

Week Thirty One
The plans
OF
the Lord
STAND FIRM
FOREVER.
PSALM 33:11

Read

Psalm 33:6–11

Remember

God promises that His heart for me won't change.

Reflect

When returning something to the store, we often check the "changed mind" box on the form. This is sometimes how we think that God operates. When we don't feel His presence, or when we've made a mistake, we fear that He will change His mind about us and reject us as His own. However, we should not forget that God promises never to change His heart towards us; we were not purchased by the blood of His Son only to be discarded like an unwanted rag doll. As His redeemed child, He always wants what is best for you. You are His masterpiece, and His purpose for your life never moves apart from His goodness.

Father, thank You. Your heart always wants the best for me.

Journal

What does the phrase "never changes" mean to me?

Pray

Praise

By the word of the
LORD the heavens were made,
their starry host by the breath of his
mouth. He gathers the waters of the sea
into jars; he puts the deep into storehouses.
Let all the earth fear the LORD;
let all the people of the world revere him.
For he spoke, and it came to be;
he commanded, and it stood firm.

The LORD foils the plans of the
nations; he thwarts the purposes of
the peoples. But the plans of the LORD
stand firm forever, the purposes of
his heart through all generations.

Psalm 33:6-11

Week Thirty Two

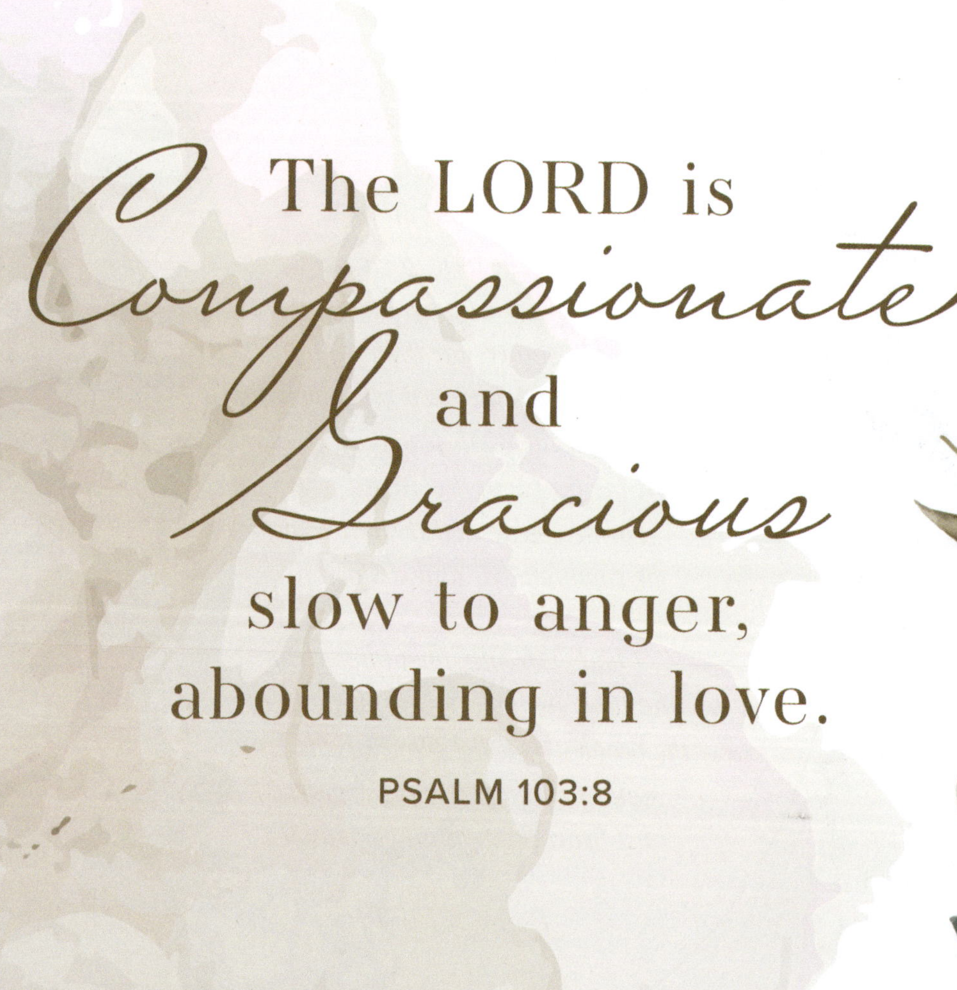

Read

Psalm 103:6–12

Remember

God promises He never runs out of mercy and grace.

Reflect

There's nothing like opening the fridge door after pouring a bowl of cereal only to find there is no milk. Similar to that feeling, we sometimes feel like our mistakes and shortcomings make us unworthy of love and grace. It's easy to feel like God works the same as the fridge, and we only get out of Him what we place in Him. But our God is not like the refrigerator or even the grocery store. His grace, mercy, and love never run out. When you make a mistake, His arms are extended regardless of your mess-ups.

Father, pour out Your compassion over me and cover my fear with Your graciousness.

Journal

What moment in my life from this past week is a beautiful reminder that God's grace is bigger than my mistakes?

Pray

Praise

The Lord performs righteous deeds
and judgments for all who are oppressed.
He made known His ways to Moses,
His deeds to the sons of Israel.
The Lord is compassionate and gracious,
slow to anger and abounding in mercy.
He will not always contend with us,
Nor will He keep His anger forever.
He has not dealt with us according to our sins,
nor rewarded us according to our guilty deeds.
For as high as the heavens are above the earth,
so great is His mercy toward those who fear Him.
As far as the east is from the west,
so far has He removed our wrongdoings from us.

Psalm 103:6-12 NASB

Week Thirty Three
God is faithful
He will not let you be tempted beyond what you can bear.
1 CORINTHIANS 10:13

Read

1 Corinthians 10:6–13

Remember

God promises He will deliver me from darkness.

Reflect

Life's deepest, darkest places are not too deep and dark for our God. You have been sought after, fought for, and bought back by Jesus, the greatest love of your life. Pitch-black darkness could not overcome His relentless love for you. When temptation knocks on your door, ask Him to show you the nearest escape. You can crush any obstacle with His strength, and with His wisdom, you can find a way out of trouble. Trust in His love and grace, and you will never be lost in the darkness.

Father, deliver me from evil and make the escape evident.

Journal

Where do you need to see God's deliverance and guidance in your life?

Pray

Praise

These things happened as a warning to us,
so that we would not crave evil things as they did,
or worship idols as some of them did. As the Scriptures say,
"The people celebrated with feasting and drinking,
and they indulged in pagan revelry." And we must
not engage in sexual immorality as some of them did,
causing 23,000 of them to die in one day.

Nor should we put Christ to the test, as some
of them did and then died from snakebites.
And don't grumble as some of them did,
and then were destroyed by the angel of death.
These things happened to them as examples for us.
They were written down to warn us who live at the end of the age.

If you think you are standing strong, be careful not to fall.
The temptations in your life are no different from what others experience.
And God is faithful. He will not allow the temptation to be more than you can stand.
When you are tempted, he will show you a way out so that you can endure.

1 Corinthians 10:6-13 NLT

Week Thirty Four

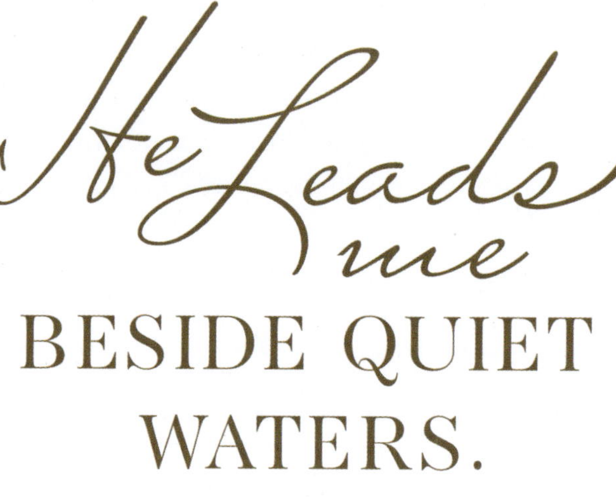

Read

Psalm 23:1–6

Remember

God promises He will lead me to rest in His love.

Reflect

The world we live in is full of noise and chaos. We often get caught up in the fast-paced routine of our daily lives without even realizing it. Our Good Shepherd doesn't demand a hurried life; in fact, He commands the opposite. Jesus places rest within our hearts so we can leave the rush behind. His provision is life-giving and restorative. When we take the time to slow down and rest in His presence, we can experience the peace and joy that goes beyond all understanding.

Father, lead my heart to quietness and give me rest.

Journal

How can I prioritize rest and quiet to allow peace and joy from sitting in Jesus's presence?

Pray

Praise

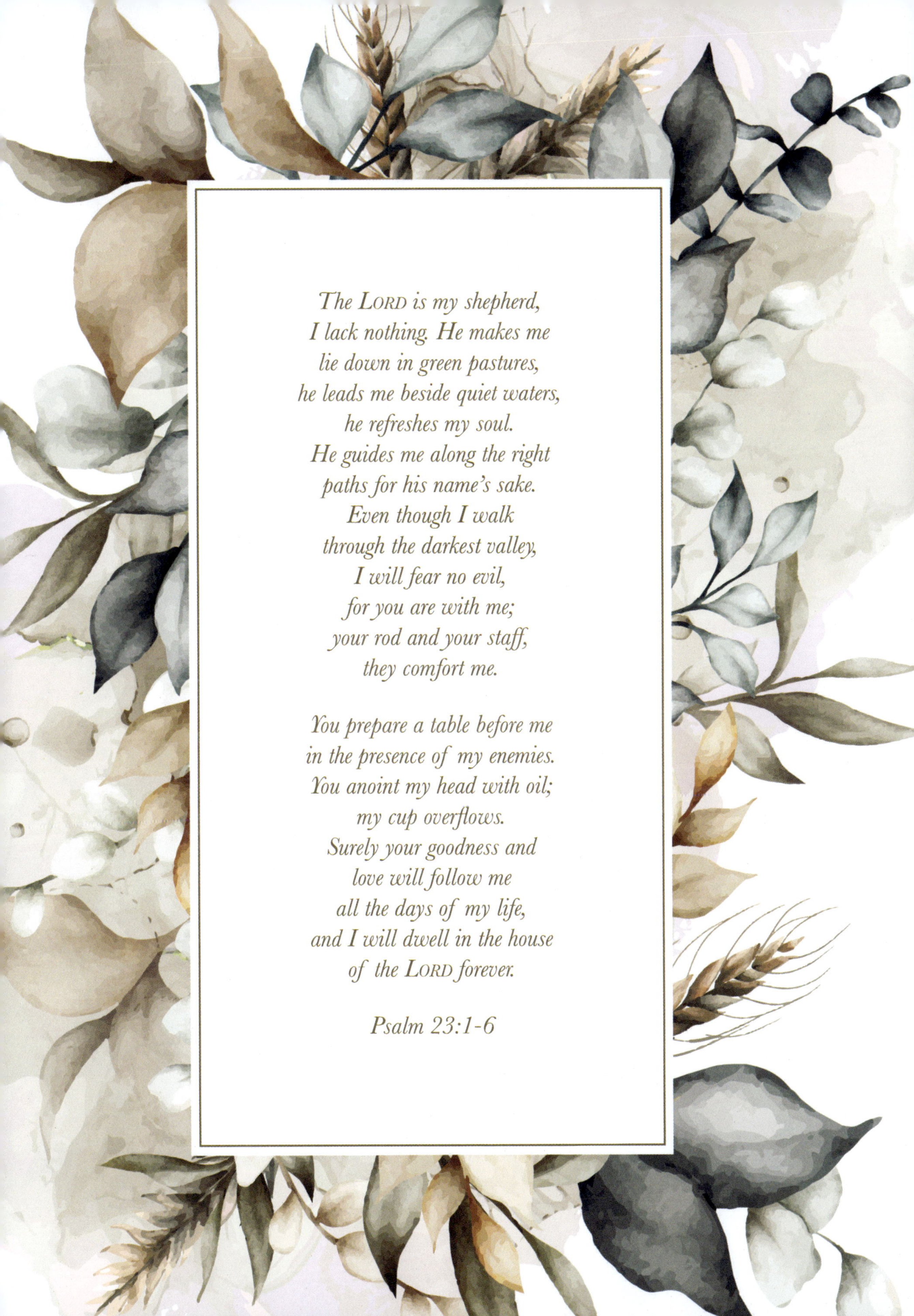

The LORD is my shepherd,
I lack nothing. He makes me
lie down in green pastures,
he leads me beside quiet waters,
he refreshes my soul.
He guides me along the right
paths for his name's sake.
Even though I walk
through the darkest valley,
I will fear no evil,
for you are with me;
your rod and your staff,
they comfort me.

You prepare a table before me
in the presence of my enemies.
You anoint my head with oil;
my cup overflows.
Surely your goodness and
love will follow me
all the days of my life,
and I will dwell in the house
of the LORD forever.

Psalm 23:1-6

Week Thirty Five
My grace
IS
SUFFICIENT FOR
YOU, FOR MY
POWER IS MADE
PERFECT IN
WEAKNESS.
2 CORINTHIANS 12:9 ESV

Read

2 Corinthians 12:1–10

Remember

God promises to give me power when I am weak.

Reflect

Struggles leave us feeling weak and ill-equipped to follow God. We're tempted to think that our inadequacies render us completely incapable of fulfilling God's plan for our lives. But the truth is, we can't live for God on our own. When we face challenges and struggles, God's grace is available to help us overcome them. Instead of hiding our weaknesses, we can embrace them, knowing that it's through our vulnerabilities that God demonstrates His power in our lives. Next time you feel weak and inadequate, remember that God's mighty power is always there to help you overcome.

Father, let my weakness be replaced with Your strength.

Journal

What weaknesses do I need to allow God's strength to overpower?

Pray

Praise

I must go on boasting. Though there is nothing to be gained by it,
I will go on to visions and revelations of the Lord.
I know a man in Christ who fourteen years ago
was caught up to the third heaven—whether in
the body or out of the body I do not know, God knows.
And I know that this man was caught up into paradise—whether
in the body or out of the body I do not know, God knows—and he
heard things that cannot be told, which man may not utter.
On behalf of this man I will boast, but on my own behalf
I will not boast, except of my weaknesses—though if
I should wish to boast, I would not be a fool, for I would
be speaking the truth; but I refrain from it, so that no one may
think more of me than he sees in me or hears from me.
So to keep me from becoming conceited because of
the surpassing greatness of the revelations, a thorn was
given me in the flesh, a messenger of Satan to harass me,
to keep me from becoming conceited. Three times I pleaded
with the Lord about this, that it should leave me.
But he said to me, "My grace is sufficient for you,
for my power is made perfect in weakness." Therefore I will
boast all the more gladly of my weaknesses, so that the power
of Christ may rest upon me. For the sake of Christ,
then, I am content with weaknesses, insults, hardships,
persecutions, and calamities. For when I am weak, then I am strong.

2 Corinthians 12:1-10 ESV

Week Thirty Six
WEEPING MAY
STAY FOR THE NIGHT,
BUT
Rejoicing
COMES
IN THE MORNING.
PSALM 30:5

Read

Psalm 30:1–5

Remember

God promises to replace my sorrow with joy.

Reflect

Today's key verse reminds us that even though we may experience sorrow, God promises to replace it with delight and awe at His work. It's easy to get caught up in our emotions and feel like we will never escape the darkness. How sweet it is to remember that the morning will come. So, when we find ourselves weeping, we can cry before our God, who considers our tears so precious. What if we anticipate the future relief, whether in heaven or on earth? You can trust in God's promise and discover hope, knowing your pain has an end. It won't last forever. God is on the throne.

Father, I give my tears to You and anticipate morning joy.

Journal

When have you endured a difficult season, how did you find hope in God's promise to transform your heartache into gladness?

Pray

Praise

I will exalt you, Lord, for you rescued me.
You refused to let my enemies triumph over me.
O Lord my God, I cried to you for help,
and you restored my health.
You brought me up from the grave, O Lord.
You kept me from falling into the pit of death.

Sing to the Lord, all you godly ones!
Praise his holy name.
For his anger lasts only a moment,
but his favor lasts a lifetime!
Weeping may last through the night,
but joy comes with the morning.

Psalm 30:1-5 NLT

Love does
not delight in
evil but
Rejoices
with
the truth
It always protects,
always trusts,
always hopes,
always perseveres.

1 CORINTHIANS 13:6-7

Read

1 Corinthians 13:4–7

Remember

God promises His love will persevere through every situation.

Reflect

As humans, we often struggle with the concept of love. It can be misunderstood, misinterpreted, and misapplied. However, the Bible clearly defines love in 1 Corinthians 13. Love is not a mere emotion or feeling, but a gift from God that always protects, trusts, hopes, and perseveres. It is a selfless and sacrificial love rooted in truth and righteousness, and He promises that love will always prevail. When your heart feels unlovely or even unlovable, embrace the promise that your God's love excels above all.

Father, let me see Your love lifting my heart above all circumstances.

Journal

How do these verses shape your definition of love?

Pray

Praise

Love is patient, love is kind.
It does not envy, it does not boast,
it is not proud. It does not dishonor
others, it is not self-seeking, it is
not easily angered, it keeps no record
of wrongs. Love does not delight
in evil but rejoices with the truth.
It always protects, always trusts,
always hopes, always perseveres.
1 Corinthians 13:4-7

Week Thirty-Eight

Every Promise HAS BEEN FULFILLED; NOT ONE HAS FAILED.

JOSHUA 23:14

Read

Joshua 23:9–16

Remember

God promises that none of His promises will ever fail.

Reflect

Sometimes, we forget God's promises will never fail. His Word assures us that not one of them will ever be broken. The Lord faithfully fulfills every promise He has made to us, and His faithfulness is evident throughout history. Joshua's farewell speech to the children of Israel charges them to remember their good God is also steadfast and committed to His word. As believers, we can trust in God's word and believe He will fulfill every promise in His perfect timing. What might happen if you prayed for fresh faith to accept God's promises and hold fast to His unfailing love and grace?

Father, give me fresh faith to believe Your promises.

Journal

Which promise of God have you been struggling to remember lately?

Pray

Praise

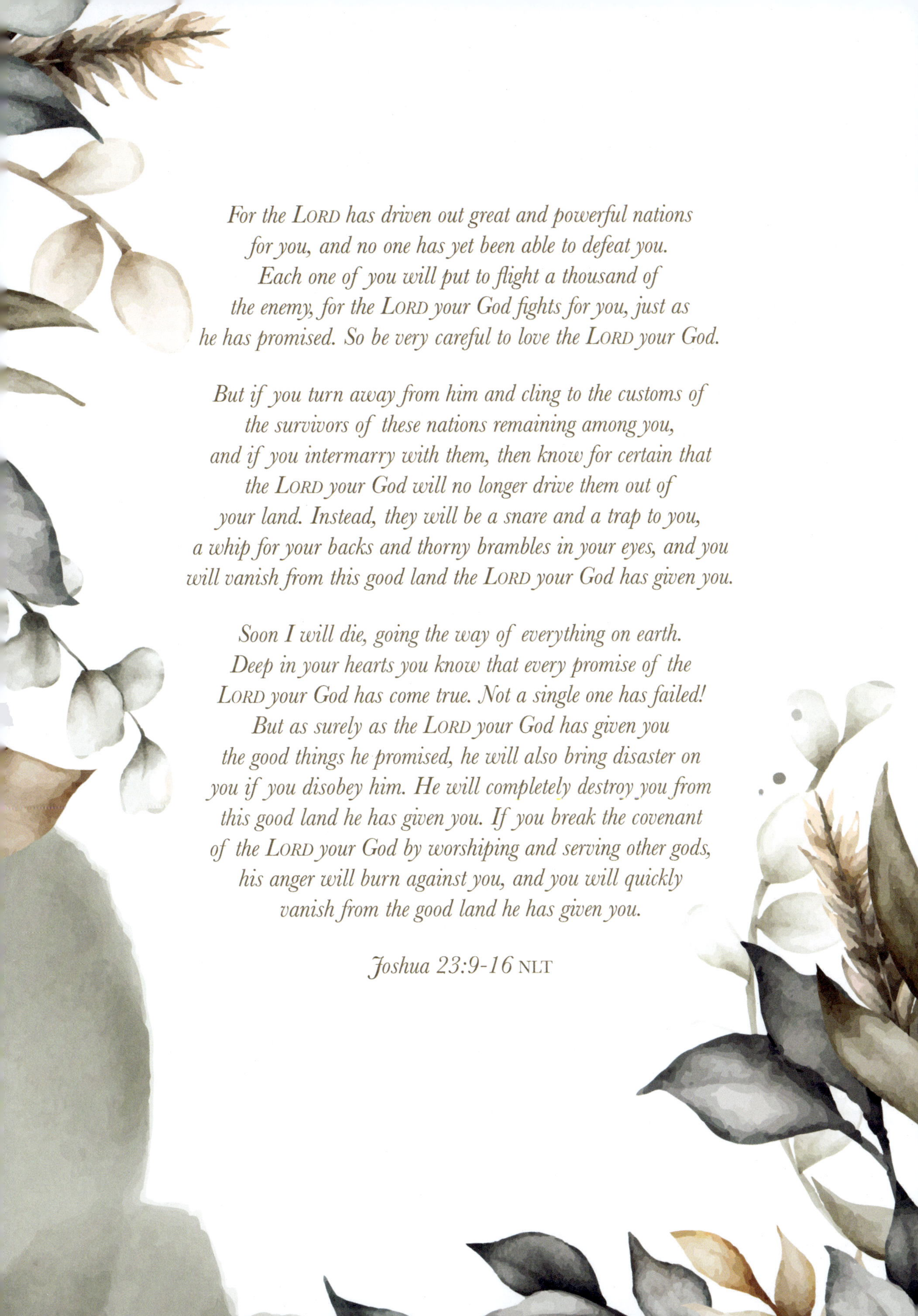

For the LORD has driven out great and powerful nations for you, and no one has yet been able to defeat you. Each one of you will put to flight a thousand of the enemy, for the LORD your God fights for you, just as he has promised. So be very careful to love the LORD your God.

But if you turn away from him and cling to the customs of the survivors of these nations remaining among you, and if you intermarry with them, then know for certain that the LORD your God will no longer drive them out of your land. Instead, they will be a snare and a trap to you, a whip for your backs and thorny brambles in your eyes, and you will vanish from this good land the LORD your God has given you.

Soon I will die, going the way of everything on earth. Deep in your hearts you know that every promise of the LORD your God has come true. Not a single one has failed! But as surely as the LORD your God has given you the good things he promised, he will also bring disaster on you if you disobey him. He will completely destroy you from this good land he has given you. If you break the covenant of the LORD your God by worshiping and serving other gods, his anger will burn against you, and you will quickly vanish from the good land he has given you.

Joshua 23:9-16 NLT

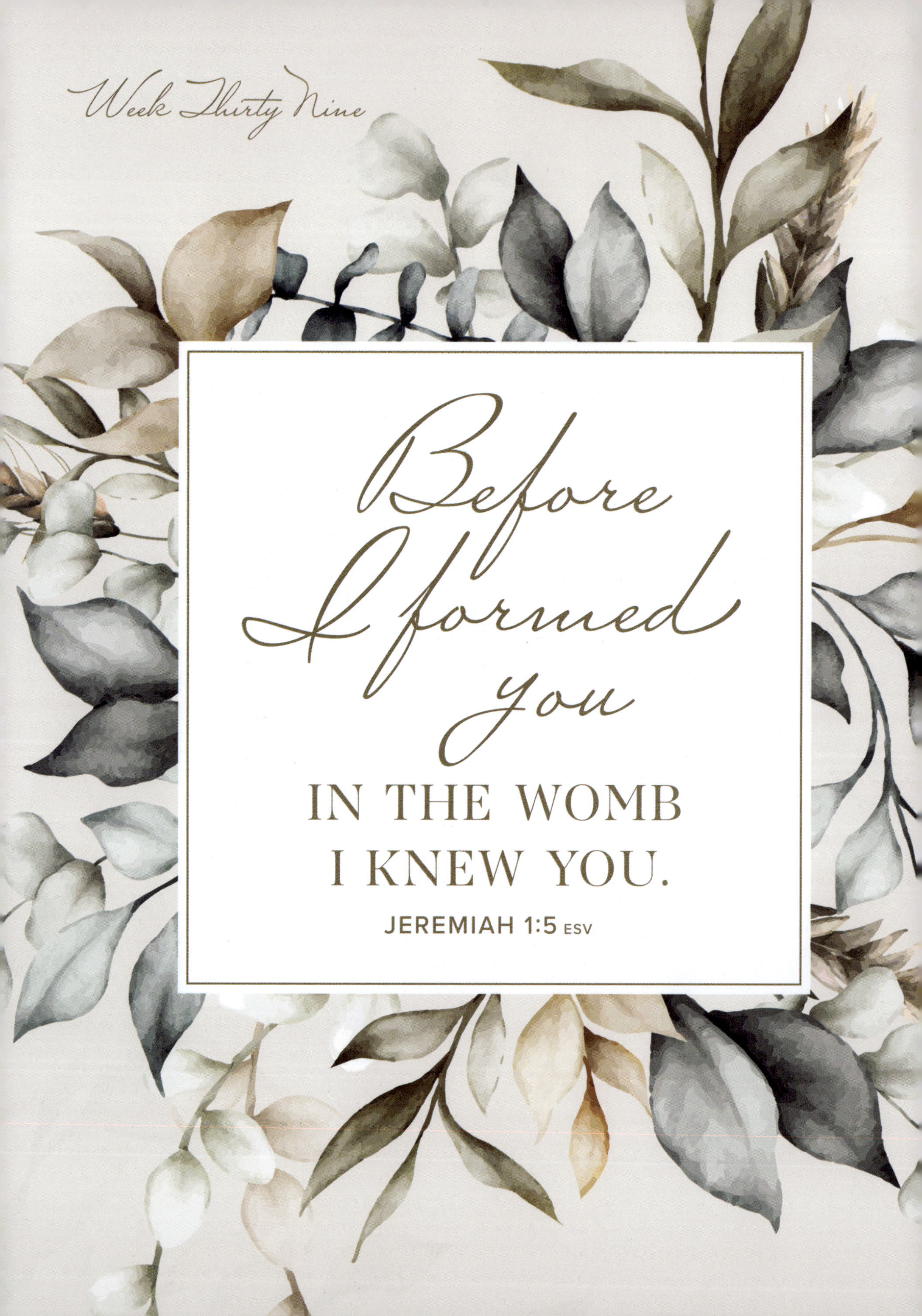
Week Thirty Nine
Before I formed you
IN THE WOMB
I KNEW YOU.
JEREMIAH 1:5 ESV

Read

Jeremiah 1:1–8

Remember

God promises He designed me for a purpose.

Reflect

If you've ever asked, "Why on earth am I here?" you aren't alone. Jeremiah 1:5 is a beautiful reminder that God has a unique design for our lives. Before birth, He knew us and set us apart for a specific task. This verse is a powerful reflection on God's sovereignty as our Creator. It's easy to become discouraged or feel lost, but this promise reminds us that we were created with a purpose. You can take comfort in knowing that God has a plan for your life and trust Him to guide you toward fulfilling that purpose.

Father, show me Your purpose for my life.

Journal

How can I find purpose in tasks I enjoy and that God has designed me for?

Pray

Praise

The words of Jeremiah, the son of Hilkiah,
one of the priests who were in Anathoth
in the land of Benjamin, to whom the word of
the LORD came in the days of Josiah the son of Amon,
king of Judah, in the thirteenth year of his reign.
It came also in the days of Jehoiakim the son of Josiah,
king of Judah, and until the end of the eleventh
year of Zedekiah, the son of Josiah, king of Judah,
until the captivity of Jerusalem in the fifth month.

Now the word of the LORD came to me, saying,
"Before I formed you in the womb I knew you,
and before you were born I consecrated you;
I appointed you a prophet to the nations."

Then I said, "Ah, LORD God! Behold,
I do not know how to speak,
for I am only a youth." But the LORD said to me,

"Do not say, 'I am only a youth';
for to all to whom I send you, you shall go,
and whatever I command you, you shall speak.
Do not be afraid of them,
for I am with you to deliver you,
declares the LORD."

Jeremiah 1:1-8 ESV

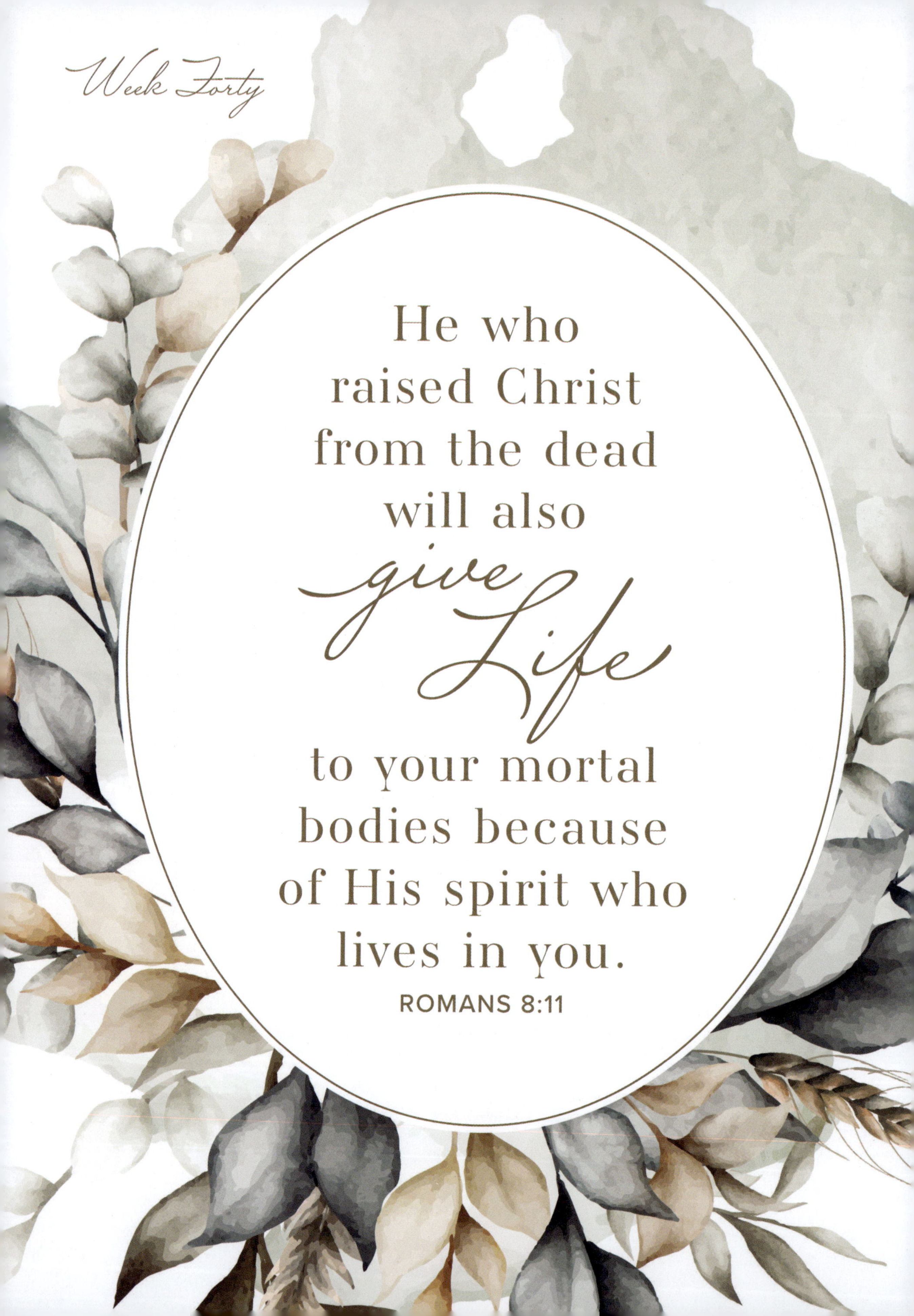
Week Forty
He who
raised Christ
from the dead
will also
give
Life
to your mortal
bodies because
of His spirit who
lives in you.
ROMANS 8:11

Read

Romans 8:5–11

Remember

God promises that the same power that raised Jesus from the dead lives in me.

Reflect

Do you ever feel like you are facing an impossible situation? The wonderful news is that, as a believer, you have access to the same power that raised Jesus from the dead. This power is not just a mere idea but a living reality. Romans 8:11 tells us that the Spirit of God, who raised Christ from the dead, is living in us, giving us strength and hope even in the darkest times. God's promise is a power that can heal our bodies, restore our relationships, and transform our lives. What might happen if you embraced this living power within you and trusted in God's promises of life and victory? You can overcome any obstacle with God's help!

Father, help me recognize that Your living power fortifies me from the inside out.

Journal

How might embracing the power of God's promises help you overcome a current obstacle?

Pray

Praise

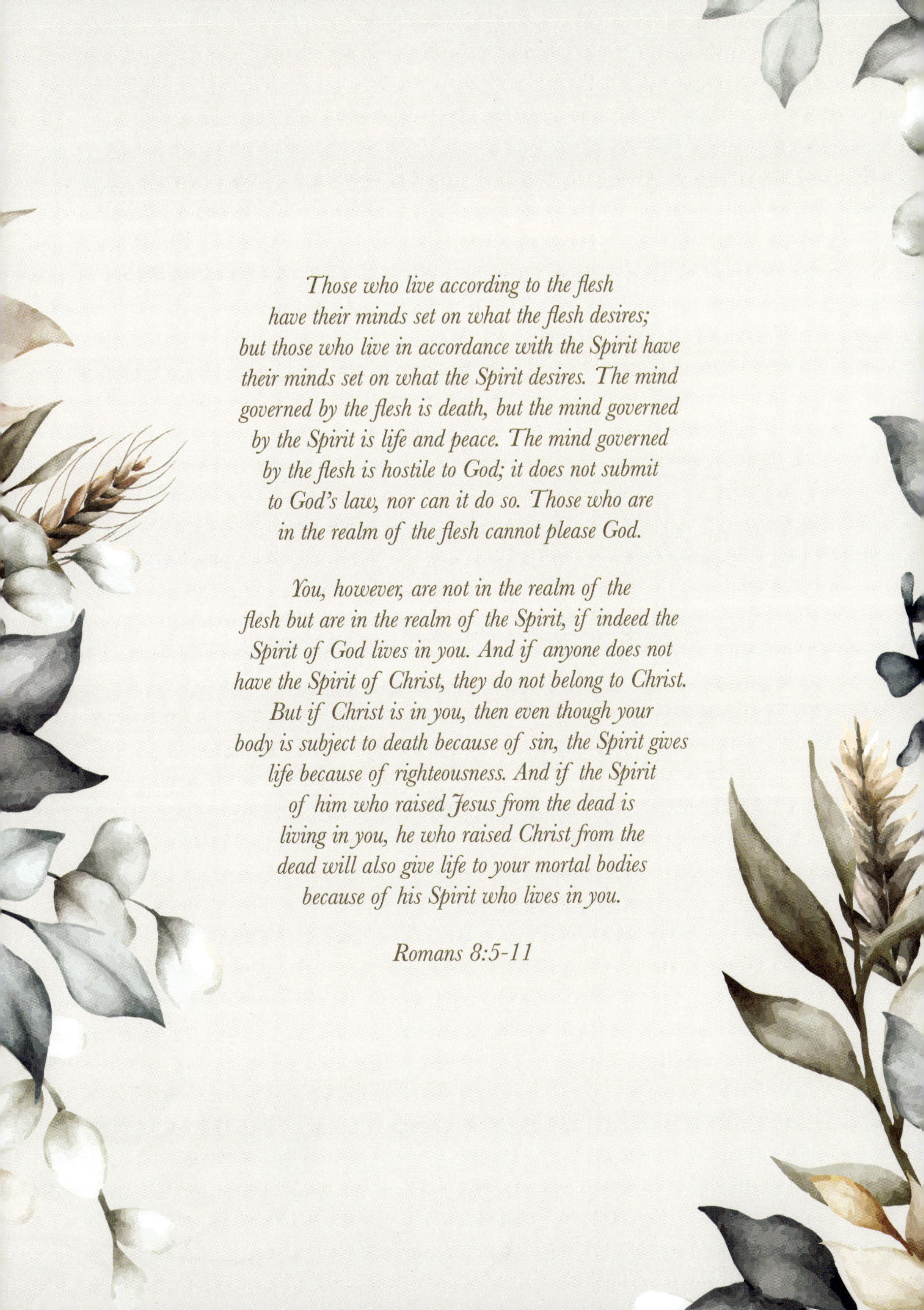

*Those who live according to the flesh
have their minds set on what the flesh desires;
but those who live in accordance with the Spirit have
their minds set on what the Spirit desires. The mind
governed by the flesh is death, but the mind governed
by the Spirit is life and peace. The mind governed
by the flesh is hostile to God; it does not submit
to God's law, nor can it do so. Those who are
in the realm of the flesh cannot please God.*

*You, however, are not in the realm of the
flesh but are in the realm of the Spirit, if indeed the
Spirit of God lives in you. And if anyone does not
have the Spirit of Christ, they do not belong to Christ.
But if Christ is in you, then even though your
body is subject to death because of sin, the Spirit gives
life because of righteousness. And if the Spirit
of him who raised Jesus from the dead is
living in you, he who raised Christ from the
dead will also give life to your mortal bodies
because of his Spirit who lives in you.*

Romans 8:5-11

The Spirit helps us in our weakness.

ROMANS 8:26 ESV

Read

Romans 8:22–27

Remember

God promises that His Spirit prays for us when we can't find the words.

Reflect

Humans often face situations where we don't know how to pray or what to say. We feel lost and helpless, unable to find the right words. But in those moments, we can find comfort in the promise that God's Spirit speaks to God the Father on our behalf. Romans 8:26 reminds us that the Spirit helps us in our weakness, praying for us with groans too deep for words. We don't have to rely solely on our own abilities, but can trust that God is with us, guiding our words and prayers. Let's recognize the power and goodness of our God, who is always there for us, even when we can't find the words.

Father, thank You for Your Spirit, praying for me when I cannot.

Journal

How has relying on God's Spirit helped you when you didn't know how to pray or what to say?

Pray

Praise

For we know that the whole creation has been groaning
together in the pains of childbirth until now.
And not only the creation, but we ourselves,
who have the firstfruits of the Spirit,
groan inwardly as we wait eagerly for
adoption as sons, the redemption of our bodies.
For in this hope we were saved.
Now hope that is seen is not hope.
For who hopes for what he sees?
But if we hope for what we do not see,
we wait for it with patience.

Likewise the Spirit helps us in our weakness.
For we do not know what to pray for as we ought,
but the Spirit himself intercedes for us with groanings
too deep for words. And he who searches hearts knows
what is the mind of the Spirit, because the Spirit
intercedes for the saints according to the will of God.

Romans 8:22-27 ESV

Week Forty Two

Come near to God

AND HE WILL COME NEAR TO YOU.

JAMES 4:8

Read

Psalm 73:23–28

Remember

God promises He will come close to me when I come close to Him.

Reflect

Have you ever gotten too busy for God? He wants to be involved in every aspect of our lives, guiding, comforting, and strengthening us. But the enemy draws us away and does everything he can to distract us away from God's presence. The promise in James 4:8 is an encouraging note to remember that while we are taking the first step toward God, He is already meeting us where we are. He will draw near to us and reveal Himself to us. Like Psalm 73 says, he holds you by your right hand. As we seek Him with a humble heart and a willingness to obey, we experience His love, grace, and mercy in new and profound ways.

Father, I praise You that Your presence is always near.

Journal

How can you actively invite God's presence into your schedule today?

Pray

Praise

Yet I am always with you;
you hold me by my right hand.
You guide me with your counsel,
and afterward you will take me into glory.
Whom have I in heaven but you?
And earth has nothing I desire besides you.
My flesh and my heart may fail,
but God is the strength of my
heart and my portion forever.

Those who are far from you will perish;
you destroy all who are unfaithful to you.
But as for me, it is good to be near God.
I have made the Sovereign LORD my refuge;
I will tell of all your deeds.

Psalm 73:23-28

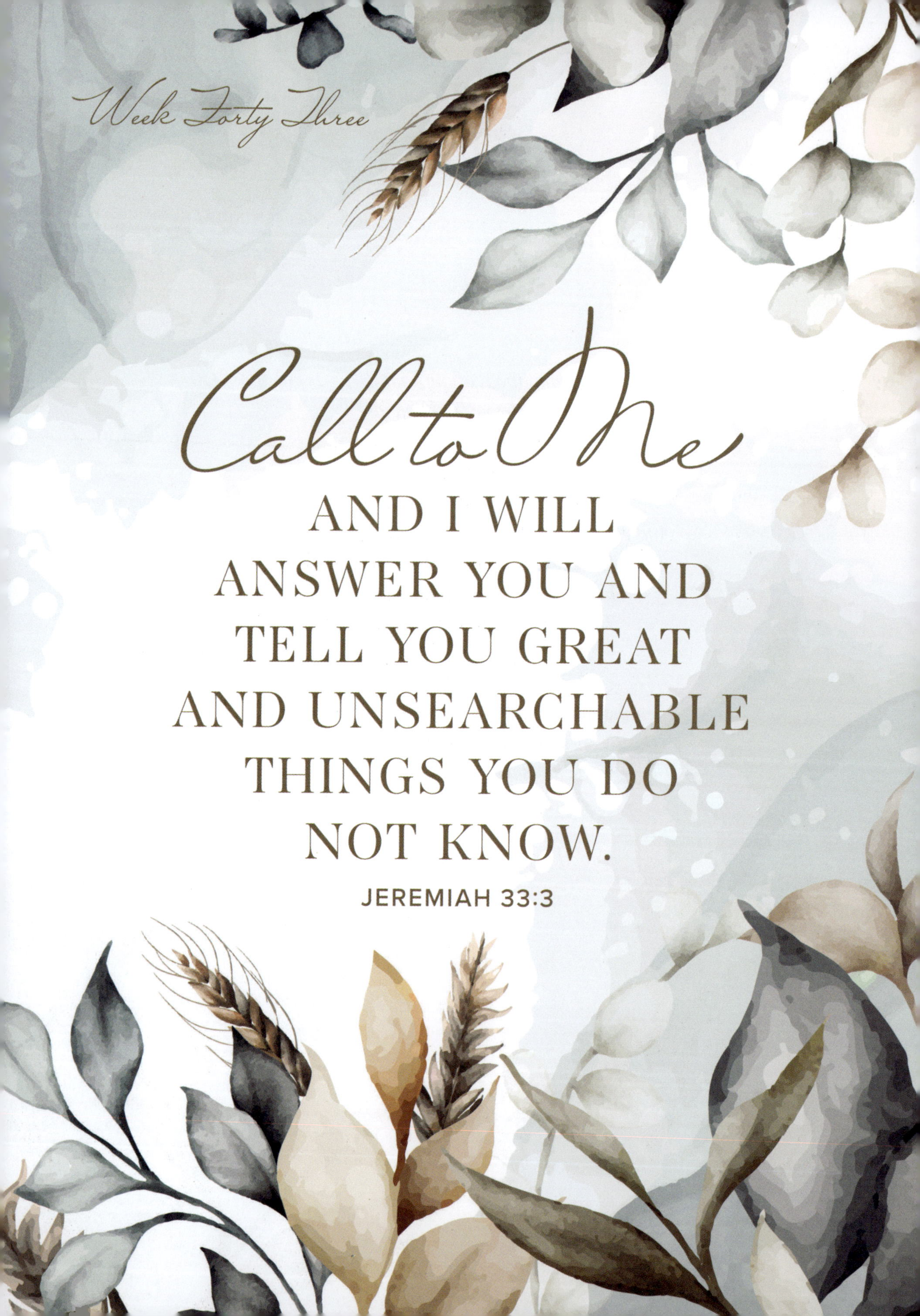
Week Forty Three
Call to Me
AND I WILL
ANSWER YOU AND
TELL YOU GREAT
AND UNSEARCHABLE
THINGS YOU DO
NOT KNOW.
JEREMIAH 33:3

Read

Jeremiah 33:1–8

Remember

God promises He will tell me incredible things when I pray.

Reflect

God's promise in Jeremiah 33:3 is a powerful reminder of the assurance we have when we pray. When we call out to God, He promises to answer us and reveal meaning and context to the issues we struggle to understand. This promise reminds us that our God is approachable and attentive to our needs. He is not distant or indifferent to our struggles and pains. In prayer, we can confidently bring our needs and requests to God, knowing He listens and responds. You can trust in God's promise to answer you when you call and expect to receive wisdom beyond your comprehension.

Father, thank You for the promise that You will noticeably respond when I call to You.

Journal

How does God's promise in Jeremiah 33:3 impact your prayer life and approach to God?

Pray

Praise

While Jeremiah was still confined in the courtyard of the guard, the word of the LORD came to him a second time: "This is what the LORD says, he who made the earth, the LORD who formed it and established it—the LORD is his name: 'Call to me and I will answer you and tell you great and unsearchable things you do not know.' For this is what the LORD, the God of Israel, says about the houses in this city and the royal palaces of Judah that have been torn down to be used against the siege ramps and the sword in the fight with the Babylonians: 'They will be filled with the dead bodies of the people I will slay in my anger and wrath. I will hide my face from this city because of all its wickedness. Nevertheless, I will bring health and healing to it; I will heal my people and will let them enjoy abundant peace and security. I will bring Judah and Israel back from captivity and will rebuild them as they were before. I will cleanse them from all the sin they have committed against me and will forgive all their sins of rebellion against me.'"

Jeremiah 33:1-8

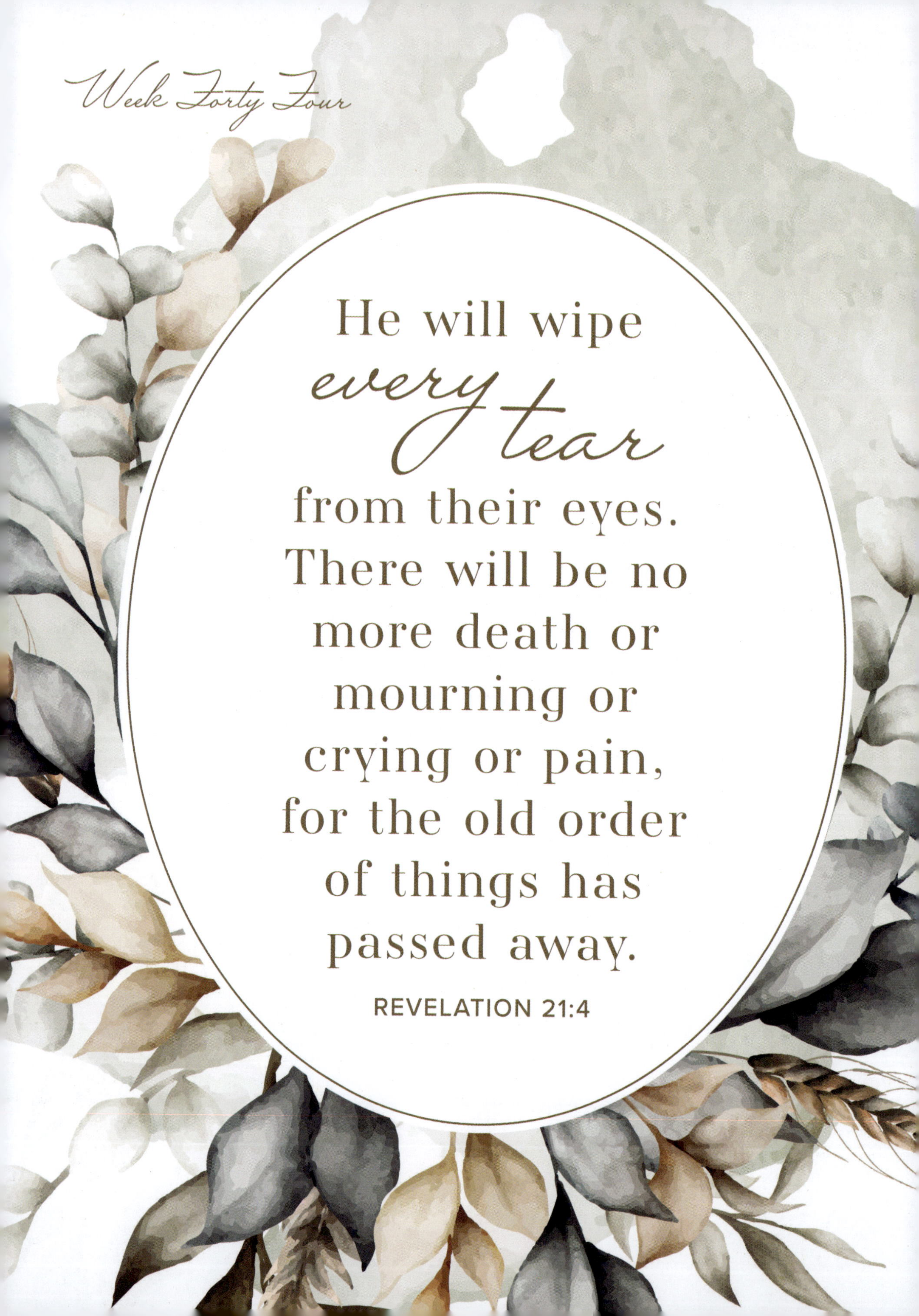
Week Forty Four
He will wipe
every tear
from their eyes.
There will be no
more death or
mourning or
crying or pain,
for the old order
of things has
passed away.
REVELATION 21:4

Read

Revelation 21:1–5

Remember

God promises one day, He will wipe away every tear.

Reflect

In this world, we experience pain, loss, and heartache that can leave us hopeless and overwhelmed. But as believers, we hold onto the promise that one day, God will wipe away every tear from our eyes. He will bring an end to all death, mourning, and pain. Until that day, we can take comfort in knowing that God sees our tears and hears our cries. We can trust Him to carry us through the difficult times and give us the strength to keep going. Let's bring our tears before Him and trust in His promise to wipe them all away one day.

Father, until the day You wipe away every tear, I give You mine.

Journal

What past or present heartbreaking circumstances do you need to lay before God and trust His promise to carry you?

Pray

Praise

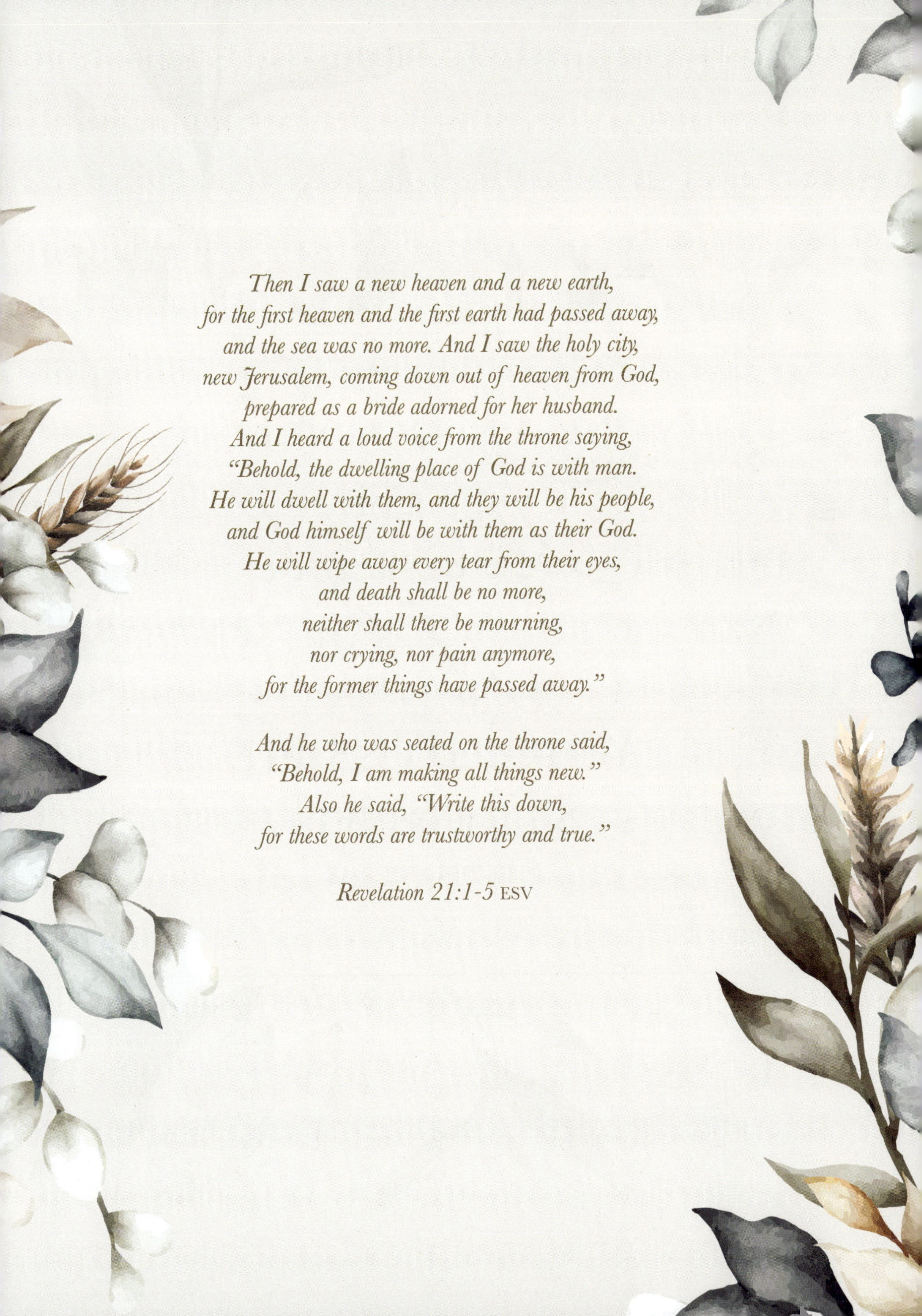

Then I saw a new heaven and a new earth,
for the first heaven and the first earth had passed away,
and the sea was no more. And I saw the holy city,
new Jerusalem, coming down out of heaven from God,
prepared as a bride adorned for her husband.
And I heard a loud voice from the throne saying,
"Behold, the dwelling place of God is with man.
He will dwell with them, and they will be his people,
and God himself will be with them as their God.
He will wipe away every tear from their eyes,
and death shall be no more,
neither shall there be mourning,
nor crying, nor pain anymore,
for the former things have passed away."

And he who was seated on the throne said,
"Behold, I am making all things new."
Also he said, "Write this down,
for these words are trustworthy and true."

Revelation 21:1-5 ESV

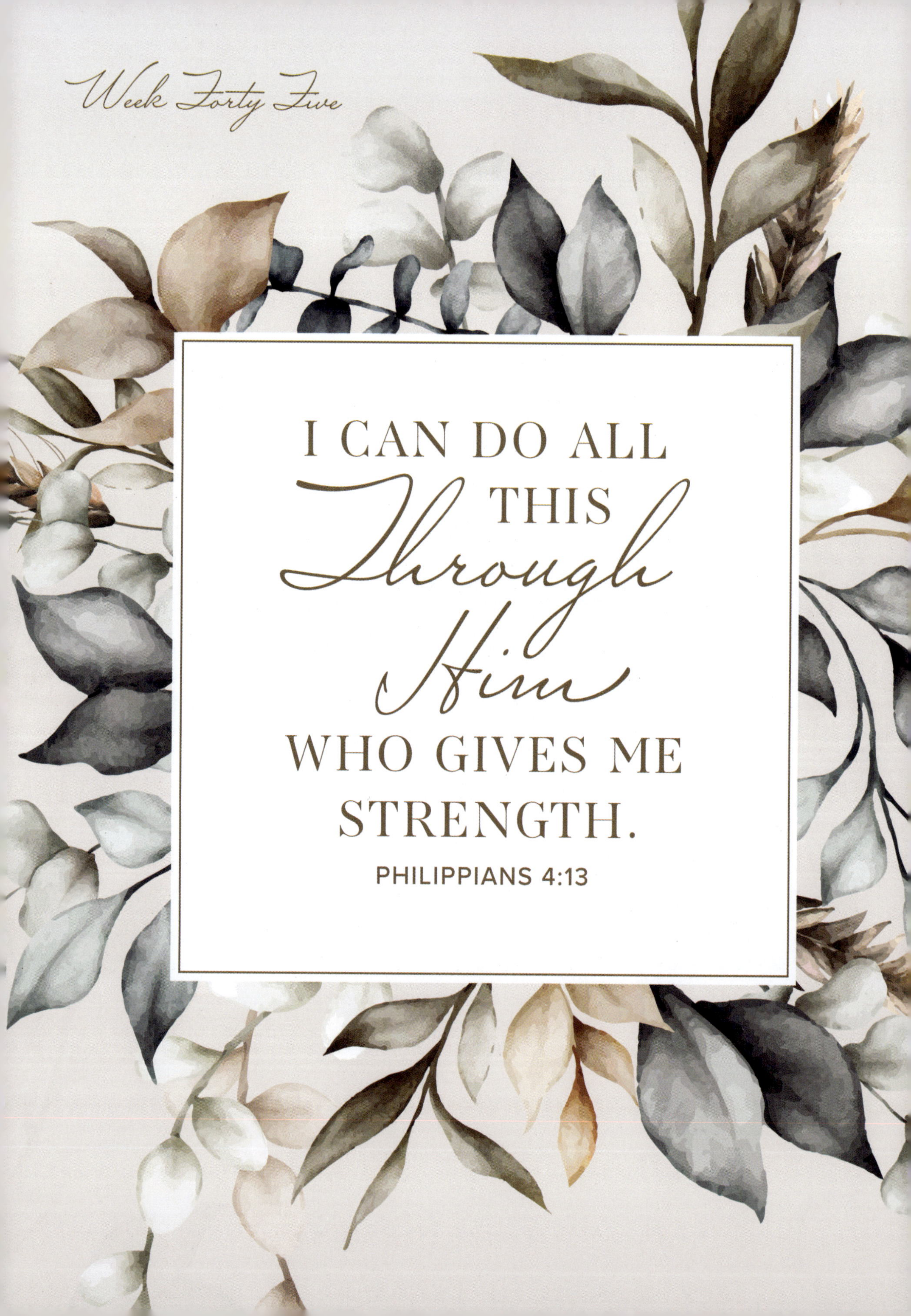
Week Forty Five
I CAN DO ALL
THIS
Through
Him
WHO GIVES ME
STRENGTH.
PHILIPPIANS 4:13

Read

Philippians 4:10–13

Remember

God promises I can do all things through His strength.

Reflect

Sometimes the seemingly simple, everyday tasks feel impossible to accomplish. Today's key verse reminds us that we have the power of God behind us, and with His help, we can conquer anything, no matter how big or small. God is large and in charge; He is bold and in control. What if you asked Him for the strength you need for today's to-do list? With His help, you can face any challenge and come out victorious!

Father, provide the strength I need for today.

Journal

How have you seen God help you complete your work by providing strength for the day?

Pray

Praise

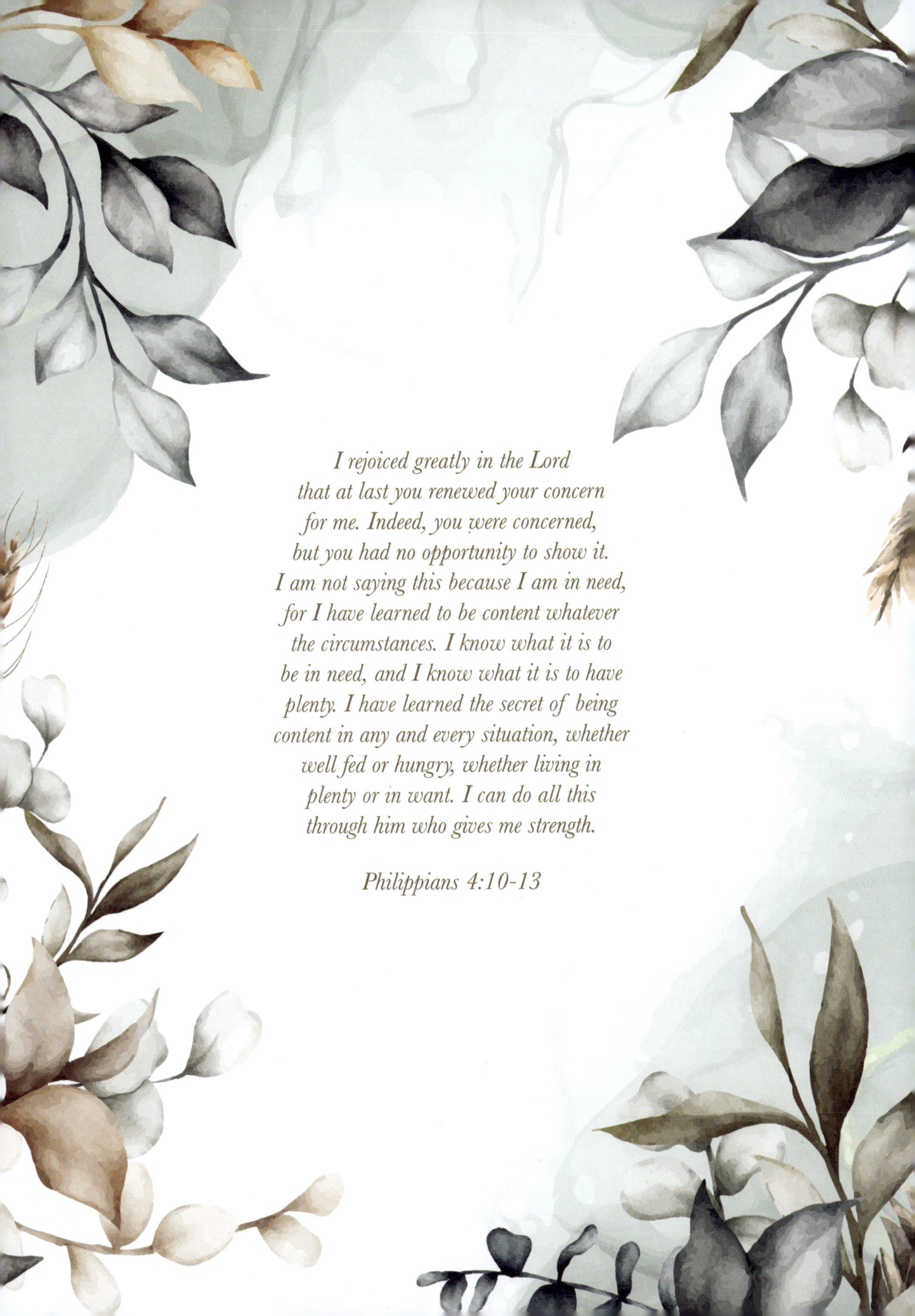

I rejoiced greatly in the Lord
that at last you renewed your concern
for me. Indeed, you were concerned,
but you had no opportunity to show it.
I am not saying this because I am in need,
for I have learned to be content whatever
the circumstances. I know what it is to
be in need, and I know what it is to have
plenty. I have learned the secret of being
content in any and every situation, whether
well fed or hungry, whether living in
plenty or in want. I can do all this
through him who gives me strength.

Philippians 4:10-13

Week Forty Six
The
LORD Himself
goes
before you
&
will be
with you.
DEUTERONOMY 31:8

Read

Deuteronomy 31:1–8

Remember

God promises He blazes the trail ahead of me and journeys with me.

Reflect

In life, we often face unknown territories and uncertain paths. But as believers, we can take comfort in the fact that the Lord Himself goes before us and journeys with us every step of the way. In Deuteronomy 31:8, God promises to blaze the trail ahead of us, making a way where there seems to be no way. He is with us always and will never leave us nor forsake us. So when fear and discouragement try to creep into your heart, remember that you can rely on God to lead you through every challenge and trial. You can trust in His promises and take comfort in His presence. God's got this!

Father, prevent discouragement from entering my heart because I rely on You.

Journal

How can you remind yourself to trust in God and rely on His promises when facing unknown territories and uncertain paths in life?

Pray

Praise

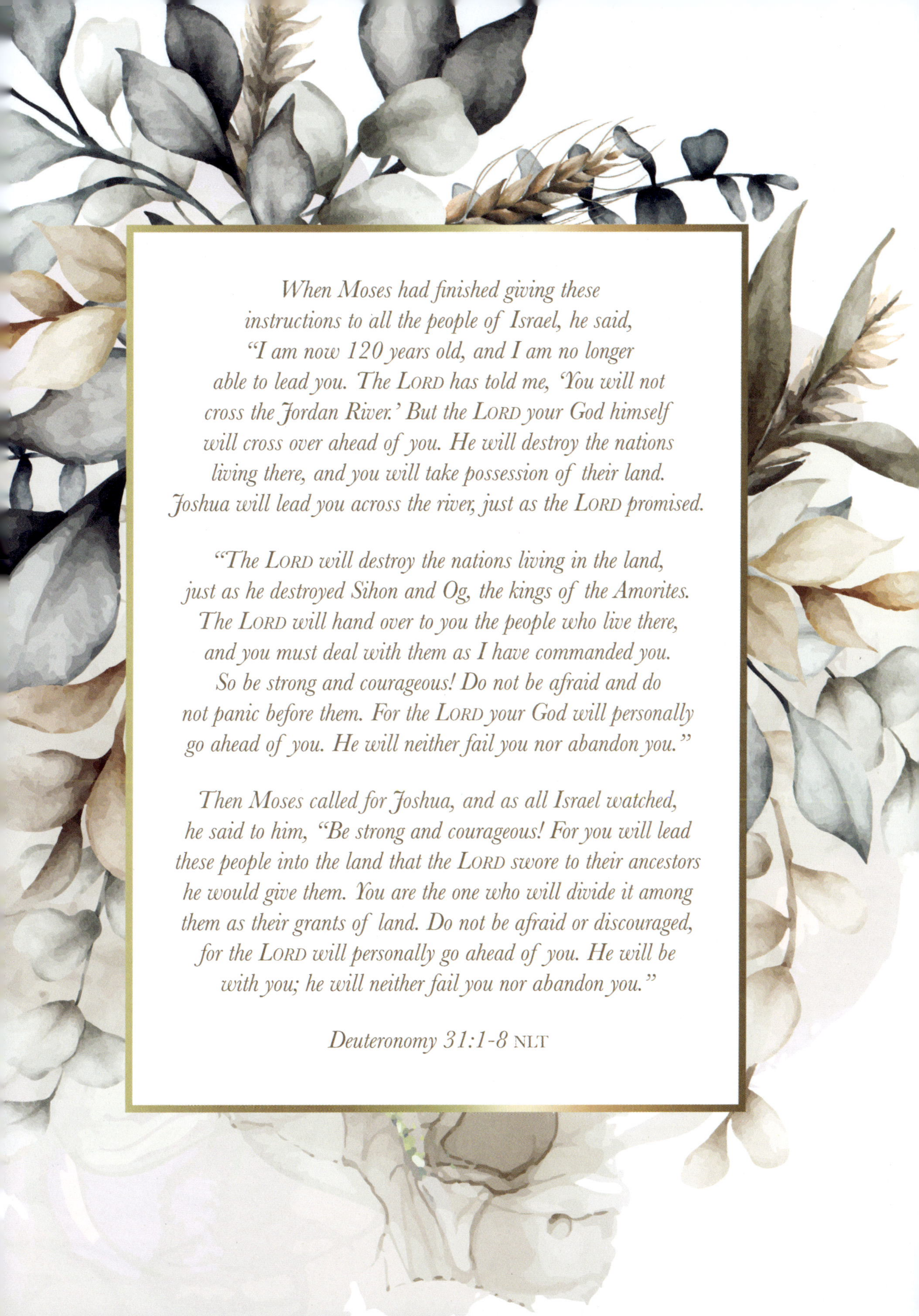

When Moses had finished giving these
instructions to all the people of Israel, he said,
"I am now 120 years old, and I am no longer
able to lead you. The Lord *has told me, 'You will not*
cross the Jordan River.' But the Lord *your God himself*
will cross over ahead of you. He will destroy the nations
living there, and you will take possession of their land.
Joshua will lead you across the river, just as the Lord *promised.*

"The Lord *will destroy the nations living in the land,*
just as he destroyed Sihon and Og, the kings of the Amorites.
The Lord *will hand over to you the people who live there,*
and you must deal with them as I have commanded you.
So be strong and courageous! Do not be afraid and do
not panic before them. For the Lord *your God will personally*
go ahead of you. He will neither fail you nor abandon you."

Then Moses called for Joshua, and as all Israel watched,
he said to him, "Be strong and courageous! For you will lead
these people into the land that the Lord *swore to their ancestors*
he would give them. You are the one who will divide it among
them as their grants of land. Do not be afraid or discouraged,
for the Lord *will personally go ahead of you. He will be*
with you; he will neither fail you nor abandon you."

Deuteronomy 31:1-8 NLT

Week Forty Seven

Read

Psalm 91:9–13

Remember

God promises His angels will guard me everywhere I go.

Reflect

The promise of God's protection provides a great source of comfort and strength for us. In Psalm 91:11, the Psalmist reminds us that God commands His angels to be our first line of defense. This promise of God's protection provides a great source of comfort and strength for us. It means we are never alone, no matter where we go or what we do. His angel army stands guard over us like a ginormous heavenly shield, reminding us that we can always trust God's love and care for us. His angels position themselves against the evil pointed our way. Take a moment today to thank God for His security.

Father, thank You for the protection of your angel armies.

Journal

How are you comforted by knowing that the angels of heaven guard you?

Pray

Praise

If you say, "The LORD is my refuge,"
and you make the Most High your dwelling,
no harm will overtake you,
no disaster will come near your tent.
For he will command his angels concerning
you to guard you in all your ways;
they will lift you up in their hands,
so that you will not strike your foot
against a stone. You will tread on the
lion and the cobra; you will trample
the great lion and the serpent.

Psalm 91:9-13

Week Forty-Eight
Blessed
ARE THOSE
WHO MOURN,
FOR THEY
WILL BE
COMFORTED.
MATTHEW 5:4 NASB

Read

Matthew 5:1–12

Remember

God promises He will comfort me when I am in mourning.

Reflect

Losing someone or something we love is one of the most painful experiences in life. It leaves us feeling alone, helpless, and overwhelmed by our grief. But in those times, we find comfort and hope in Jesus by holding on to His promises. He promises to be with us always, to comfort us, and to heal our broken hearts. His love and mercy are never-ending, and we discover peace and solace when we open our hearts to Him. You can trust that He will guide you through your suffering because He has promised.

Father, I need Your comfort in the mourning spaces of my heart.

Journal

What grief spaces need to open for Jesus' healing to enter?

Pray

Praise

Now when Jesus saw the crowds,
He went up on the mountain;
and after He sat down,
His disciples came to Him.
And He opened His mouth and
began to teach them, saying,

"Blessed are the poor in spirit,
for theirs is the kingdom of heaven.
Blessed are those who mourn,
for they will be comforted.
Blessed are the gentle,
for they will inherit the earth.
Blessed are those who hunger
and thirst for righteousness,
for they will be satisfied.
Blessed are the merciful,
for they will receive mercy.
Blessed are the pure in heart,
for they will see God.
Blessed are the peacemakers,
for they will be called sons of God.
Blessed are those who have been
persecuted for the sake of righteousness,
for theirs is the kingdom of heaven.

"Blessed are you when people insult you
and persecute you, and falsely say all kinds
of evil against you because of Me.
Rejoice and be glad, for your reward in
heaven is great; for in this same way they
persecuted the prophets who were before you."

Matthew 5:1-12 NASB

Week Forty Nine
God is Love
WHOEVER LIVES IN LOVE LIVES IN GOD, AND GOD IN THEM.
1 JOHN 4:16

Read

1 John 4:7–21

Remember

God promises His love is dependable.

Reflect

It's easy to doubt the reliability of love in a world where it's often fleeting. But, as Christians, we can find comfort in God's promise that His love is dependable. We can trust in His love for us, as He is love, and whoever loves lives in God, and God lives in them. It's amazing to be loved by the Creator of the universe! So, let's praise Him for His faithful love, which endures through all circumstances. What might happen today if you could strive to love others as He loves you and, by doing so, live in the presence of God's love? Oh, how He loves you.

Father, I praise You for loving me faithfully, no matter what.

Journal

How might your day change if you chose to live in God's love and longed to love others as He loves you?

Pray

Praise

Dear friends, let us continue to love one another, for love comes from God. Anyone who loves is a child of God and knows God. But anyone who does not love does not know God, for God is love.

God showed how much he loved us by sending his one and only Son into the world so that we might have eternal life through him. This is real love—not that we loved God, but that he loved us and sent his Son as a sacrifice to take away our sins.

Dear friends, since God loved us that much,
we surely ought to love each other.
No one has ever seen God. But if we love each other,
God lives in us, and his love is brought to full expression in us.

And God has given us his Spirit as proof that we live in him and he in us. Furthermore, we have seen with our own eyes and now testify that the Father sent his Son to be the Savior of the world. All who declare that Jesus is the Son of God have God living in them, and they live in God. We know how much God loves us, and we have put our trust in his love.

God is love, and all who live in love live in God, and God lives in them. And as we live in God, our love grows more perfect. So we will not be afraid on the day of judgment, but we can face him with confidence because we live like Jesus here in this world.

Such love has no fear, because perfect love expels all fear. If we are afraid, it is for fear of punishment, and this shows that we have not fully experienced his perfect love. We love each other because he loved us first.

If someone says, "I love God," but hates a fellow believer, that person is a liar; for if we don't love people we can see, how can we love God, whom we cannot see?
And he has given us this command:
Those who love God must also love their fellow believers.

1 John 4:7-21 NLT

Week Fifty

See,
I have
Engraved
you
on
the palms of My
hands; your
walls are ever
before Me.

ISAIAH 49:16

Read

Isaiah 49:14–18

Remember

God promises He has carved my name in His palm.

Reflect

Have you ever noticed a piece of jewelry or décor with engraving? The etching on an object often explains the significance of it. Isaiah 49:16 emphasizes we are so important to God that He has engraved us on the palms of His hands. He considers our lives to be so valuable that He carries us with Him. When we feel lost or alone, we can take comfort in knowing that God cares for us deeply. He's still got the whole world in His hands. Let Him guide you through life's challenges, knowing your name is forever etched into His hands and heart.

Father, show me how precious I am to You.

Journal

How can you remind yourself daily that you are important to God?

Pray

Praise

But Zion said, "The LORD has forsaken me, the LORD has forgotten me."

"Can a mother forget the baby at her breast and have no compassion on the child she has borne? Though she may forget, I will not forget you! See, I have engraved you on the palms of my hands; your walls are ever before me. Your children hasten back, and those who laid you waste depart from you. Lift up your eyes and look around; all your children gather and come to you. As surely as I live," declares the LORD, "you will wear them all as ornaments; you will put them on, like a bride."

Isaiah 49:14-18

Week Fifty One
GOD IS
OUR
Refuge
+
Strength
AN
EVER-PRESENT
HELP IN
TROUBLE.
PSALM 46:1

Read

Psalm 46:1–11

Remember

God promises to support us through every circumstance.

Reflect

Have you ever read a headline that left you rejoicing because of good news? God's promises hold wonderful news for us. While the world is full of troubling situations, God is our ever-present help in trouble. No matter what we face, we can take comfort in His persevering power. He promises to help us in times of trouble, and we can trust in His unfailing love and faithfulness. When discouragement lurks, or trouble haunts us, we can turn to God and seek His help. He's with you every moment of every day; you can rest in this promise!

Father, give me eyes to see how You are helping me right now.

Journal

How can you embrace God's promise to be your ever-present help in your current set of circumstances?

Pray

Praise

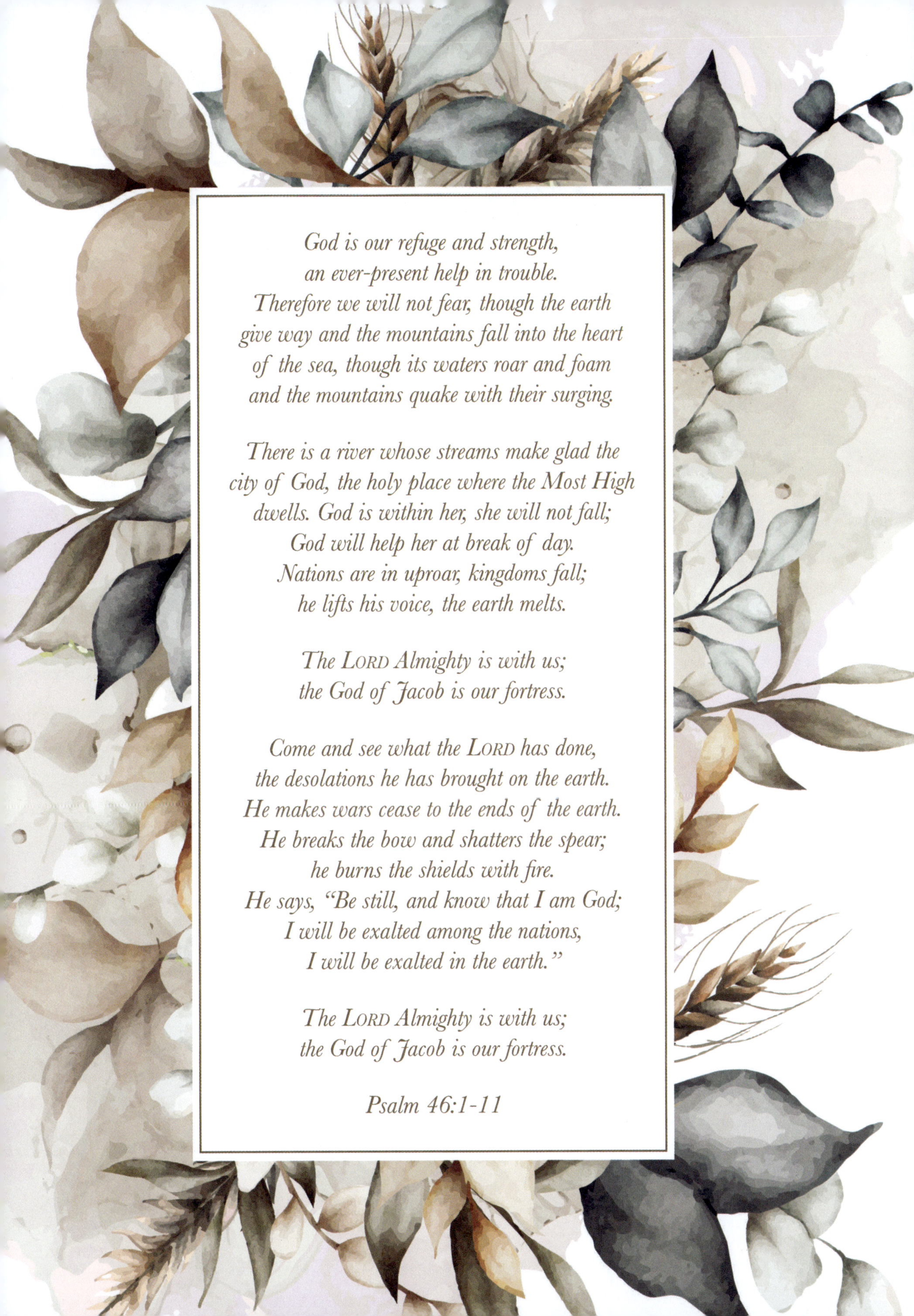

God is our refuge and strength,
an ever-present help in trouble.
Therefore we will not fear, though the earth
give way and the mountains fall into the heart
of the sea, though its waters roar and foam
and the mountains quake with their surging.

There is a river whose streams make glad the
city of God, the holy place where the Most High
dwells. God is within her, she will not fall;
God will help her at break of day.
Nations are in uproar, kingdoms fall;
he lifts his voice, the earth melts.

The LORD Almighty is with us;
the God of Jacob is our fortress.

Come and see what the LORD has done,
the desolations he has brought on the earth.
He makes wars cease to the ends of the earth.
He breaks the bow and shatters the spear;
he burns the shields with fire.
He says, "Be still, and know that I am God;
I will be exalted among the nations,
I will be exalted in the earth."

The LORD Almighty is with us;
the God of Jacob is our fortress.

Psalm 46:1-11

Week Fifty Two
The name of
the LORD is a
fortified tower
the righteous
run to it
and are safe.
PROVERBS 18:10

Read

Psalm 18:1-5

Remember

God promises His name is a strong tower for my safety.

Reflect

Proverbs 18:10 acts as a GPS verse, guiding the way. This passage tells us if we're on the run, let's run to Jesus. The name of the Lord is not just a word or a phrase, but His name represents His character and power. We can depend on Him and find refuge in Him. When we face challenges or difficulties, we can call out to the name of the Lord and find safety and security in Him. Trust in the name of the Lord and run to Him in every situation. He will protect you and keep you safe; that's His promise.

Father, thank You for keeping me safe in Your arms, and for securing my heart with Your name.

Journal

How has trusting in the name of the Lord provided safety and security for you in difficult times?

Pray

Praise

I love you, Lord, my strength.
The Lord is my rock, my fortress and
my deliverer; my God is my rock, in whom
I take refuge, my shield and the horn
of my salvation, my stronghold.

I called to the Lord, who is worthy of praise,
and I have been saved from my enemies.
The cords of death entangled me;
the torrents of destruction overwhelmed me.
The cords of the grave coiled around me;
the snares of death confronted me.

Psalm 18:1-5

ANSWERED PRAYERS

Prayer Request:____ **Date:**__________

Prayer Request:____ **Date:**__________

Prayer Request:____ **Date:**__________

Prayer Request:____ **Date:**__________

Prayer Request:____ **Date:**__________

Prayer Request:____ **Date:**__________

Prayer Request:____ **Date:**__________

ANSWERED PRAYERS

Prayer Request:____ Date:__________

____

____

Prayer Request:____ Date:__________

____

____

Prayer Request:____ Date:__________

____

____

Prayer Request:____ Date:__________

____

____

Prayer Request:____ Date:__________

____

____

Prayer Request:____ Date:__________

____

____

Prayer Request:____ Date:__________

____

____

ANSWERED PRAYERS

Prayer Request:______________________________ **Date:**________

Prayer Request:______________________________ **Date:**________

Prayer Request:______________________________ **Date:**________

Prayer Request:______________________________ **Date:**________

Prayer Request:______________________________ **Date:**________

Prayer Request:______________________________ **Date:**________

Prayer Request:______________________________ **Date:**________

ANSWERED PRAYERS

Prayer Request:____ Date:____________

____

____

Prayer Request:____ Date:____________

____

____

Prayer Request:____ Date:____________

____

____

Prayer Request:____ Date:____________

____

____

Prayer Request:____ Date:____________

____

____

Prayer Request:____ Date:____________

____

____

Prayer Request:____ Date:____________

____

____

ANSWERED PRAYERS

Prayer Request:____________________________________**Date:**__________

Prayer Request:____________________________________**Date:**__________

Prayer Request:____________________________________**Date:**__________

Prayer Request:____________________________________**Date:**__________

Prayer Request:____________________________________**Date:**__________

Prayer Request:____________________________________**Date:**__________

Prayer Request:____________________________________**Date:**__________

ANSWERED PRAYERS

Prayer Request:______________________________ **Date:**__________

____

____

Prayer Request:______________________________ **Date:**__________

____

____

Prayer Request:______________________________ **Date:**__________

____

____

Prayer Request:______________________________ **Date:**__________

____

____

Prayer Request:______________________________ **Date:**__________

____

____

Prayer Request:______________________________ **Date:**__________

____

____

Prayer Request:______________________________ **Date:**__________

____

____

ANSWERED PRAYERS

Prayer Request:____**Date:**__________

Prayer Request:____**Date:**__________

Prayer Request:____**Date:**__________

Prayer Request:____**Date:**__________

Prayer Request:____**Date:**__________

Prayer Request:____**Date:**__________

Prayer Request:____**Date:**__________

ABOUT THE AUTHOR

Rachel Wojo is an author, public speaker, and podcaster who hosts Bible reading challenges on her popular blog, rachelwojo.com. Her biblical approach and life circumstances influence women to find strength and hope in everyday situations. Rachel's journey includes losing her mother to leukemia, her adult special needs daughter to a rare neurologically degenerative disease, and her father to illness. She is the author of *One More Step: Finding Strength When You Feel Like Giving Up* and *Desperate Prayers: Embracing the Power of Prayer in Life's Darkest Moments*. Mostly, Rachel is crazy in love with Matt, mom to six on earth and two in heaven.